Manna:
Unleash the Ride.
International
Motorcycle
Shows.Com [2013-2014]

Volume 21

QUEEN OLYMPIA VICTORIA

authorHOUSE®

AuthorHouse™
1663 Liberty Drive
Bloomington, IN 47403
www.authorhouse.com
Phone: 833-262-8899

Published by AuthorHouse 06/06/2022

ISBN: 978-1-6655-6150-1 (sc)
ISBN: 978-1-6655-6149-5 (e)

CONTENTS

Introduction vii

Chapter 1   Stop The Presses! 1
Chapter 2   Baksheesh Versus Bilious 18
Chapter 3   Dreams Really Do Come True! 34
Chapter 4   Mr Sketch Scented 56

Conclusion 69
A Proclamation! 73

INTRODUCTION

The wise man Solomon once said that where there is no vision the people perish, but he that keepeth the law, happy is he. Satan the great apostate and deceiver would have us believe that breaking the law and disregarding the precepts of God would make us happy, enlightened, evolved beings. Nothing could be further from the truth as those who embrace the devil's philosophy generally end up perishing as fools.

We are standing on the threshold of great and solemn events and the final movements will be rapid ones. Whither bound mankind? I believe I was born for such a time as this to receive messages from heaven to share with the world to guide them to safety before the great conflagration of earth sets in. To this end I have faithfully chronicled every experience and vision to bring hope and inspiration to a dying world. The other day in a dream, I was standing in the woods at a fork in the road, when I looked to my right and saw a dark lonely road winding uphill on a steep incline. To my left I saw another steep uphill road but as I looked to the sky I saw the radiant sunshine appearing all of a sudden and it grew brighter and brighter, scattering rays of splendor all around. I stood entranced at the sight and took in every moment of the scene until it disappeared. This dream is a breakthrough dream holding the promise of freedom, happiness, joy and rest!

Today, Sabbath May 7, 2022 my husband and I went to church and were blessed. We watched a clip promoting the new evangelistic program for the church under the acronym T. M. I For the Adventists, it stands for *TOTAL MEMBER INVOLVEMENT*. The clip featured Pastor Ted Wilson and Mark Finley and others giving an evangelistic promotion, but it had no audio so we could not hear what was said. The silence was well served because it seemed as if God were saying to them, you had *too much information for you to be attempting The Mission Impossible* at this late hour. Your program without the message of the hour and without present Truth is an exercise in futility!

The microphone with audio was then transferred to the Layman's Movement at that very hour. We shouted in our spirits and gave God the praise!

CHAPTER ONE

STOP THE PRESSES!

———◦◦◦◦———

Earthly governments are patterned after the heavenly government in heaven and the law of heaven governs both jurisdictions. In the same way the I. R. S and F. B. I agencies operate on earth, it's the same way they operate in the spiritual realm. I ordered an F. B. I T-shirt on Amazon to indicate the inspection phase of the judgment. The "Great Dick" is at the Governor's mansion as a Porter at the door to expel the unkempt ones and to retain the kempt ones who have on the robe of Christ's righteousness. "The night is far spent, the day is at hand: let us therefore cast off the works of darkness, and let us put on the armor of light. Romans 13:12

Wise rulers will not permit the people to be oppressed because of the envy and jealousy of those who disregard the law of God. All need to keep eternity in view, and not to act in such a way that God cannot ratify their judgment in the courts of heaven.

HEALING THE PARALYTIC. JOHN 5.

In John 5. Christ turns up at the Pool of Bethesda and finds a paralytic man lying helpless for 38-years. He asked the man a question: "wilt thou be made whole?" The man replied that he had no one to put him in the pool when the angel troubled the water so he was always left behind. Jesus then told the man to take up his bed and walk and he did so and was healed. And

1

the day was the Sabbath day. The female version to this story is declared in this fashion.

So, in the fullness of time, Jada Pinkett Smith, Pris (daughter-in-law) and I were at the pool of Bethesda at Walmart on aisle A-1 38 waiting for the angel to trouble the water. Christ appeared to Lady P. and asked, "wilt thou be made whole?" She immediately responded that she was blessed and highly favored and was quite alright. She was whole and perfect in her eyes and needed no help. So, Christ decided to leave with the kingdom in His hands when I saw what happened and [I] shouted out the opposite. I said, Rabboni, we are broken and depressed!!! Immediately Jada responded that we needed sexual healing! I gave Jada the side- eye and told her that we are supposed to be virgins, professing a pure faith. (Revelation14.) She said that she had heard Daniel the prophet say that Michael shall stand up at the time of the end to deliver and he seems to have a magnum! (Daniel 12:1) I then told her I did not want her to spoil my beautiful daughter-in-law. Suddenly, we heard Michael say, "Your wish is my command. What's on your bucket list?"

In a flash Will Smith stood up, and Will. i. am said Amen! Will then proceeded to the Oscar stage and slapped Chris Rock so hard that water gushed out that night. But the taste was not the taste of water but the taste of aged wine! Once he returned to his seat the Rock said that there was honey flowing abundantly too, so the Fresh Prince announced that the tarrying period was over (Matthew 25) and now it's the Honeymoon time! The Psalmist said that we are to open our mouths wide and God will fill it. He will fill our mouths with laughter and joy and good things. The earth however, is getting her mouth opened wide so that she can swallow the unbelieving ones who will enter the bowels of the earth and be cut off forever.

Our thirst and hunger have now been assuaged and we praise our Creator. And so, Pris in due time delivered Prince Shiloh to the world and made me a grandma thrice over. Amen. At this time the patrons at the Oscars gave King Richard a standing ovation and 49ers Colin kaepernick took a knee! We bow down and worship the King of Kings.

IN THE SHADOW OF THE MARK OF THE BEAST SYSTEM.
Revelation 13.

"In the great final conflict, Satan will employ the same policy, manifest the same spirit, and work for the same end as in all preceding ages. That which has been, will be, except that the coming struggle will be marked with a terrible intensity such as the world has never witnessed. Satan's deceptions will be more subtle, his assaults more determined. If it were possible, he would deceive the very elect." G. C (Introduction) xi.

The time is fast approaching when many will urge the enforcement of Sunday worship as an observance that will greatly improve the morals of society. Thus the fourth commandment, the observance of the seventh-day Sabbath will be cast away and the law altogether.

The template for the Mark of the Beast system was created by the first F. B. I director, J. Edgar Hoover under the caption Coin-Tel-Pro. The coin refers to the currency in the image beast (666) and the *tel* refers to the entelechy of the organism. In time, the features of the religio-political system will develop into global mandates. Right now it is in the tadpole stage of development. The *tel* also refers to a christian named Telford who represents the development of a sealed people who will counteract the forces of the beast system and be as saviors to the nations around. (144,000 living saints). The *pro* refers to the word proscribe or prohibit. You will be prohibited from buying or selling unless you have the mark on your hand or in your forehead.

So, when Ben Carson of the tribe of Benjamin bought a table set for his HUD office to the tune of $31,000, he was using the beast number just as Michael Cohen did in his $131,000.00 payment to Stormy Daniels. When Ben misspelled the word Proverbs on his shrine it was a hint that the Proscription was about to take place. He erected a plaque on which were the names of proscribed traitors. Hence the fear of the overturn of Roe vs. Wade at the Supreme Court level runs deeper than a spermatozoa and an ovum, as they could use the same laws to perform citizen's arrest on those who refuse to disobey God's law. It would appear to all involved that we are viewing the amphibian stage of this system when Meghan Markle, Duchess of Sussex had to flee the Frogmore palace to the safe hills of California to preserve her sanity. This system is not a simple system.

In 2006, when Trump raised an 80-ft flagpole at his Mar-a -lago estates, it indicated that Mystery Babylon, the Mother of Harlots was about to come on the stage of action. That incident occurred 16-years ago. In 2006, Twitter was created, the Pittsburgh Steelers won the Superbowl and the crocodile hunter was killed by a stingray.

All the world is in a state of agitation at this time and politicians can more easily prey on the people. A crisis is upon us and the work must be done speedily. The reason that Lisa Hanna the politician lost to Mark Golding in the 2019 Party elections was due to the fact that the age of the beast is ripe and the beauty must give way to the head of gold on the Mark of the beast, Mark Golding.

The Image Beast system has a base of operation in the Immigration system where the brother /sister filing was recently changed from a period of 10-years to 13-years. God is ready to gather the saints from the four winds and transport them to the land of our fathers. Satan wants to hinder this process by preventing God's people from receiving the seal thus he is creating a system to keep them in bondage to Babylon. He wants them to get a mark of dishonor instead of the high mark of approval. The address at 1925 Brickell Avenue in Florida has 92 years of darkness in the middle, which is the allotted time for the "night of sin." The Brickell name denotes those who worship after the order of Cain-a false worship at the brick altar, while the "Ke in the middle of the name" denotes those who worship at the true altar of stone like faithful Abel. The name Rodney and Bernstein Immigration group shows that God's eternal Truth in the form of the Rod will be preserved for the people. The true people of God will feast on butter and honey once the impenitent ones are removed from their midst and they are no longer commingled. "Mindy" relates to the two kinds of minds in the world-the mind of God that bear the stamp of pure, straightforward, unswerving integrity; and the mind of Satan and satanic agents who confederate to oppose the building up of the kingdom of God. Tony Bent, an immigration lawyer in Florida, represents those who bend under the chastening hand of God and do not rebel, but pass under the rod and are saved. The other set will bow down and bend under the weight of sin to the Image Beast and receive the mark of perdition. Such ones will burn in a lake of fire prepared for the devil and his angels. Revelation.

THE FLINTSTONES AND THE JETSONS.

The wise virgins took extra oil with them which denotes the individual's reservoir of Truth in action. The foolish virgins were satisfied with the Truth they had acquired while joining the church that bore the message of the Judgment for the Dead, but failed to acquaint themselves with the additional message-the message of the Judgement of the Living.

"These were left out with the tares only because they let the Devil sow in their hearts seeds of foolishness, seeds of contentment (lukewarmness) with the initial truths by which they joined the church; thus they mistakenly felt no need for additional light from the Lord. But when prophecy began to fulfill itself beyond the scope of Divinely revealed knowledge, and as they saw the events of the gospel shaping themselves contrary to their expectations, they become alarmed and confused, saw themselves in darkness. The lesson is unmistakable. Those who for ever feel "rich and increased with goods, and in need of nothing" more, will not get to the "door" on time.

Timely Greetings, Vol. 1. #21 pg7

The SDA church was turned into the Flintstones when the "door" was shut on the unfaithful ones in April, by L. P They are assembled on Flint-Stone Mountain (Hwy-78) with Barney, Wilma and Bam-Bam. The Five wise virgins are with the Jetsons-Elroy, Judy, Rosie and Astro, on Mt. Rushmore, filled with the Holy Ghost.

IRAN HOSTAGE CRISIS. [1980]

GOT OIL? I JUST RAN OUT OF OIL. CAN YOU GIVE ME SOME?

Those who run out of oil in the crisis will have to go back in search of oil. They go back to President Jimmy Carter the #39th president who warns them against selling the soul for peanuts on the plains of Dura! The Eagles Rock Studios on Jimmy Carter Blvd. reveals the fate of those on whom the Rock falls because the eagles are ready to have a party. [Luke 17]. There are many who will follow unsound doctrines to the detriment of their souls, leaving off the good golden oil to take in substitutes of grease. (John Travolta-Grease (1978)) Get off Satan's enchanted ground before it is too late-The church of Scientology Organization.

The ones who escape go forward to meet the 40th President Ronald Reagan, who announces Morning in America to the faithful. We shout out "Eureka" because we found the Promised Land near Kings Row at the Milk'n Honey restaurant on Wesley Chapel Road. The studio for the born again ones is the Black Lightning Studios on Snapfinger Drive. God's amazing grace will definitely lead us home!

THE SEALING TIME IS OVER.

The miracle of the fish with a coin in its mouth to pay the temple taxes is a reflection of what will happen in the end time. A pisces woman will head to the IRS to collect the seal of the living God for the 144,000 living saints in the time of the end. The IRS issued the first bill for $152.32 and asked the following questions: Are you still hitched to the grisled horses on the chariot of Zechariah 6? [No]

Are you lukewarm? [No]

Are you of the order of Mahershalalhasbaz, born only once? [No]

Having received the negative responses, they sent out a different bill for $120.50 with different questions.

Are you loosed to take the Bay chariot of Zechariah 6 into all the world? [Yes]

Are you hot? [Hotter than hot]

Are you of the order of the Emmanuelites? [Yes]

The other two seal offerings totalled $159.00 and took us to Christine King-Farris and Bernice King at the King Center.

Three fresh offerings amounted to another $27.00 that brought the grand total of the seal to $86.00. The Kingdom sign. Christ took 27 giant steps in all to rescue us from the pit in the month of April. The "fool" was born on April 1, while our Savior was born on April 3. He then took 16 steps to dismantle the underworld at the cross, [3+16=19] Once He rescued us He took 8 more steps to lead us into the Promised Land and secure our eternal salvation. [19+8=27] That is why my email is wjudy127@gmail.com because we are sealed with the angel guard. 100+27 means the Lamb is standing on Mt. Zion and with Him are 144,000 living saints. The number 186 therefore references the total number of years that the sanctuary process consumed to fulfill the great transaction. Therefore the Lamb (100) with the Kingdom (86) total 186 years. 1844-1930-2016. [86+86=172 years]. I have an epilay with the Approval notice from heaven determining that the group of sealed ones number 144,000 saints with an angel guard around them. Revelation 14. We are therefore heading toward the period of the "High Winds."

The seal of destruction for the wicked in the church totals 670 points. This seal is a combination of i-75 in Georgia and i-595 in Florida. Our Mercedes Benz tag is RTK 6757. That means Returning King -67 [lost ones] taken out from the first fruits (57) in a 10-degree turn. In 2006 the Pittsburgh Steelers won the SuperBowl with a perfect score of 21 points. They beat the SeaHawks by 11 points.

SUNDAY MAY 8, 2022. IT IS DONE. IT IS DONE. IT IS DONE. TIME: 6:03 AM.

The SDA church has been weighed in the scales of the sanctuary and has been found wanting. The scores had been ratified at the Nissan stadium in Tennessee with the playoffs between the Titans and the Houstons. The Titans represent the wise virgins who have the extra oil, while the Houstons represent the foolish virgins who ran out of oil.

In the playoff games, November 2019 at Nissan stadium, the Houstons won against the Titans with a score of 24-21. In December 15, 2019 the Titans won against the Houstons in a tough match-35-14.

	1	2	3	4	T.
Titans	7	7	7	14	35
Houston's	7	0	7	0	14

When the spiritual IRS got the scores they reviewed them and issued a notice of deficiency for the Houston's and a notice of approval for the Titans. Ancient Israel was given the Oracles of God [7] but despised the Messiah and crucified Him so they ended up with zero. [0] Modern Israel was again entrusted with the Oracles of God [7] and they too despised the messengers and rejected the kingdom message. So, they too are left with a zero and no kingdom to gain, [0]. They like Achan of old coveted the goodly Babylonish garment by ridiculing the dress reforms and pouring contempt on the health reforms by despising the sacred restrictions. So Brian Flores of Dolphins fame took the numbers (670) to the Pittsburgh Steelers in the north who had won Super Bowl 2006 with a perfect 21 score. The FBI told him to saddle number 24 with the sin for the scapegoat sacrifice. Brian detected that one as the person asking for oil, having run out of gas. So it turned out that Dwayne Haskins was found wanting and died at age 24 on interstate i-595 searching for gas. He wore number 7. Under the 7th seal, the sinners are taken out of the congregation in the spiritual garbage truck. All junk was removed by the Stand-up Guys and the church delivered! To ascertain that the job was completed, Christine King -Farris turned 94 years to confirm that the spell over the human family was forever broken at last. [94-24=70]. The spell is over! Hurrah, Hurrah!

Farris-King is an alumni at Spelman College in Atlanta. We are victorious today.

JAMAICA AT 60 YEARS. THE MARRIAGE SUPPER OF THE LAMB. THE YEAR OF JUBILEE.

When Jamaica celebrates her Diamond jubilee in August, 2022 it will be a celebration of the end of sin in the church. Sin has run its course and the temple is cleansed. We are now on the pages of Revelation in chapter 22. Glory, Hallelujah. We are to celebrate this event with the Bridegroom who has come back to deliver the kingdom to us. A kingdom of mortals will inherit Palestine to showcase God's truth and righteousness to the world. To this end I pray that ambassadorial visas be granted my family and I so that we can attend the Grand Gala at the National Stadium on this auspicious occasion for we are indeed ambassadors of Christ from the commonwealth of Israel.

When Hugh MacKintosh Foot [Lord Caradon] former governor of Jamaica turned 115 years in the grave, Jamaica would have been delivered. (2022) We have seen the Savior's foot [Foot], we have seen His face, [cara] and we have heard His voice in the Obligation of Optimism. Jerusalem our happy home has been restored to us. This mighty nation then is to proclaim liberty to all the oppressed nations that God is inviting them to a kingdom of peace where there will be no more homelessness or poverty or violence. And Jada's hair will grow back! Every man will be under his own fig tree and there will be even a covenant of peace between the animals.

The Twins

Jenna and Barbara Bush took us from the Burning Bush through Tia and Tamera, the Gorman twins, the Thorpe twins and finally the Clayton twins who Jacob talked about in Genesis 49. Tia represented the loss of the kingdom and Tina represented the restoration of the kingdom with the letter N in her name! [8+6=14] Mr. Levell has leveled the playing field for us so that we can chase the devil off the planet and ban him from the universe as we protest the evils of the world and "chant down Babylon. And there will be no more haves and haves not. Thank God!" Pat Tillman of the Arizona Cardinals fame is the till that gives the holy ones a song in their hearts. This #40 is a sign that we out of the desert and have gotten the victory. Sin has no more dominion over us. Tillman and Haskins were given the seal for the lost ones as they were taken out mysteriously by "friendly fire." Meanwhile Ronald Reagan #40 and Oprah Gail Winfrey are the custodians of the seal for the righteous. God will not rest till He make Jerusalem a praise in the earth. While there are five symbolic months to the slaughter of Ezekiel 9 according to Brother Houteff (July -November) there are seven literal months to the

Great Disclosure in the Great and Dreadful Day (May -November). Hence we get the Mayflower in May and Thanksgiving in November.

"MOVE FRAM YASSO." WE HAVE COME FULL **O**.

"Move fram yasso;" means "Let there be light." In the beginning God said, let there be light and there was light. Genesis. He says so again at the end of time in the Revelation.

God allowed the United Nations and her allies to drift into the arms of Putin and the Ukraine war because America has turned her back on God who has blessed her above all nations. She has turned her back on God who alone can help her. Now is the time to return to God and repent. Study the message of the hour so that you can get the seal of the living God and come under divine protection.

Follow us on Facebook and Twitter and subscribe to our You-Tube channel *ONE WORD ADVENT MINISTRIES*. THIS IS IT! The death knell is already sounding in the position of N. E. L at the Snellville church and the middle name of Ruby Nell Hall, nee Bridges.

AMEN AND AMEN. HALLELUJAH.

MONDAY MAY 9, 2022. THE SUN HAS SET ON THE SDA CHURCH OF LAODICEA. "CASKETS FOR ADVENTISTS"-ADS

So, when the grim reaper Ted Cruz discovered that the Laodiceans were feeding on milk doctrines he told Broderick Harvey who immediately complained to Trump about the rebellious ones who refused to pass under the Rod. Steve Harvey had a check in his possession that labeled a leader in the congregation as a hypocrite, living in the darkness of this world. #7414 for $592.00, written on April 1, 2022. Trump got very alarmed because he knew that milk kept at lukewarm temperatures was subject to temperature abuse. This condition of being neither cold nor hot causes pathogens to proliferate and cause death. So he enlisted Cruz's help to take the contaminated ones to Mexico to the Sierra Madre mountains where they were to be cut down as trees that cumbereth the ground. (Luke 13). These Sierra Mountain ranges are like spiritual lumberjacks that take out the spiritual junkies from our midst. Ted Cruz then reported the mission accomplished although he was berated for leaving Texas during a winter storm to visit Cancun.

Thanks be to God. We say Thy will be done on earth as it is done in heaven, O Mighty One.

Trump wants to buy Real Estate. Greenland. [Denmark].

Code: A Green Landfill.
Marjorie Taylor-Greene is the embodiment of that green landfill for the unbelieving ones in the church whose carcasses fell in the wilderness on the very borders of the Promised Land. So, thus far we see that the signs of the impending judgment are not spiritual but real. God's wrath on the wicked is always a literal vengeance.

Psalm 58:10 "The righteous shall rejoice when he seeth the vengeance: he shall wash his feet in the blood of the wicked.

So that a man shall say; Verily there is a reward for the righteous: verily he is a God that judgeth in the earth.

Thanks be to God. Amen.

Amen.

Time: 6:57

The Grease Monkey is Here!

Malachi 3&4. The Lord comes suddenly to His temple. A grease monkey is a mechanic especially one who works on automobiles and airplanes. In slang terms it is a slightly built burglar with entry skills. Right now by heaven's light we have seized the darkness. We found his house and Flintstone mountain. (4182 Indian Manor). We got his license plate number-AFM 4182 and his checkbook. #7414.

"Behold I come quickly, hold fast till I come."

So, the day K and Kev. joined the Frugals team was the day we beat the darkness "street and lane." The Grease Monkey came in and crashed the Oscars and the Grammys, and the Narwhals created quite a commotion from then onwards!

Amen 🙏.

Today May 11, 2022.   Time: 10:44 AM

Starburst. Take Charge and Mean IT. Turn "can do" into "can did." You got IT in you!. It's Yours For the Taking!

READY TO GO RADIOACTIVE! TOOT! TOOT!

THE STAR-SPANGLED BANNER IS THE SWAN SONG OF THE LAODICEANS; THEIR FINAL ANTHEM.

My brother in Florida sent me this trivia last week that I found quite interesting as the war numbers relate to the kingdom sign of 6+8 =14. Take a look.

Start date: 28-7-1914
28+7+19+14=68

World War 11
Start date: 01-9-1939
01+9+19+39 =68

World War 111
Start date: 24-2-2022
24+2+20+22=68

Some may wonder if this is mere coincidence but I think it is Providence at work in gathering the people of God from the four winds of the earth. It is the truth that will gather the people as they respond to its charms and sweet music. My address at 34 River Road, Decatur Ga. 30034 is the embodiment of truth as it incorporates the 3-fold truth and the 4-fold truth in double sentiments. **34+34=68.** That perfection has come is reflected in a current monthly rental of $600.00 which represents 6000 years of human probation. Thus we are at the end of our physical journey, about to embark on the supernatural leg of our odyssey to home. God intends to use the war to clear the land for the second exodus of His faithful believers. It is time to revolutionize the entire landscape and fill Jerusalem with holy people who can be an example of godliness in the earth. So I say to the unbelieving Jews and unconsecrated Arabs in the land: AWAY WITH "DA" WAILING WALL. GET OFF ABRAHAM'S LAND! MOVE FRAM YASSO. THE SWORD OF THE LORD AND OF GIDEON. "BLOOD, FIRE, AND BRIMSTONE!"

NO MORE STINGER!

"RADIO" AND THE YELLOW JACKETS AT GA. TECH.

James "Radio" Kennedy's story seems to be one of God's amazing grace towards fallen man. Although mentally disabled he was very fond of football at his TL Hanna High school and would accompany the team to games. He always carried a radio transistor with him as his favorite gadget. The Yellow Jackets sting of sin brought death and ruin to the human race but Jesus stooped very low to lift up the fallen race to restore us to radioactive status! Radio would walk around with a trolley of gifts to hand out at Christmas time in the neighborhood. How thoughtful of him to do so. There is a sign coming soon that tells me there will soon be no haves and haves not in God's kingdom because the God of heaven will restore every one under his own fig tree. There was a time when the team left Radio behind and the team lost 21-27 to the rival team. They never left Radio after that loss as they went on to win 13 straight games thereafter. He was like their lucky charm! And so our Lucky Charm has taken His 27 steps to liberate us from sin and sinners so we must give Him all the glory and all the praise.

THE MAYFLOWER AND OPRAH WITH MR. FLORES.

And so, in the fullness of time Brian Flores was summoned to the Nissan Stadium in Tennessee where he saw Oprah and the spirit of Ronald Reagan rejoicing with great joy. They were shouting hallelujah because they had overcome the world, the flesh and the Devil. Oprah was given the $86.00 seal of approval to keep for the 144,000 and she eventually settled in Canaan at the behest of Jehovah Nissi. When Oprah was given the seal, she was told it also represented the 5th parabolic year from 2016-2021 when Joe Biden would sign Juneteenth into law, as a Federal holiday, setting the spiritual captives free! Oprah was satisfied that she along with the faithful were finally welcomed into the **BELOVED** and Gail, her best friend was right beside her. (Song of Solomon)

Then Brian turned to a different scene and heard the U. S anthem playing for the Laodiceans. But it had a very strange tune just like Luther Strange 111 in Alabama. "O, say can you see O foolish Laodiceans how you have bartered away your salvation! Who hath bewitched you into believing that the 144, 00 is a symbolic number and that the slaughter of Ezekiel 9 is not literal? Whoever tricked you into believing that there is not to be a kingdom in Palestine but that you are headed to the pearly gates in heaven? Those immensely expensive hot -air balloons would surely bankrupt hell in Albuquerque. Cheaper to remain where you are!

Like the Star spangled banner, please remain where you are.

Brian was then given the numbers to give Dwayne Haskins of Pittsburgh fame which meant judgment and sure destruction. Brian said to God, "Who, me?" I cannot bear such numbers because they are too heavy for me. "So he left the Pats domain and Tennessee and fled to Florida where he began swimming with the Dolphins. Little did he know that the start of the 5th symbolic year for the Laodiceans was given in 2017 when the Dolphins beat the Falcons -20-17 in the playoffs. (2017-2022). On November 20, 2017, the Georgia Dome imploded and the falcons escaped to their new home at Mercedes Benz stadium.

But Brian complained bitterly in his spirits about the task at hand because it was a crazy idea to believe a loving God would destroy his creation in a slaughter. The church people have always said that God is too merciful to visit His people in judgment and they were good Adventists. However

Dolphins top brass sensed that Brian was too much of a burden to the Franchise especially since the Nissan car was sent to Winter Gardens Fl. to indicate that the winter has started and the Laodiceans were not saved. Then it was that Brian got fired and God told Goodell not to hire him for the Giants because Brian has a Pitt stop to make in Pittsburgh. When Brian got wind of the double deal with another Brian he got angry and sued the NFL and the Farmer in the Dell Goodell.

Still determined like Jonah to evade his responsibility, Flores looked to Texas Head coach for some LOVE but he was rebuffed, so guess where he found refuge? Yes, in Pittsburg, with the Pittsburgh Steelers. Indeed the temple has to be cleansed and it will be. Yesterday my husband finally cut off the limbs off the tree that was overhanging the house. It is a work of retribution that will finally get the Lord's house in order and reestablish order and discipline for all.

And so, Haskins who went a-asking for gas on i-595 brings the curtain down on the Laodiceans' false worship in the house of God. Their worship is almost like that of Eric Garner peddling cigarettes on the New York shop plaza with flinty foreheads!

A great reunion is about to take place. Amen.

FRIDAY MAY 13, 2022.   TIME: 11:03 AM
LOTTO FRIDAY.

"The old Devil well knows that this is the last message the world will ever receive and that it will chain him for a thousand years, and at last reduce his being down to ashes as though he never was. Therefore he is like a "roaring lion seeking whom he may devour." Symbolic Code 182, Vol. 2. Nos. 3. 4 p. 4

The kingdom though wrapped in splendor, has a messy job to do on arrival for the cleansing of the temple, so to this end it comes to town with a Dumpster marked 9915068, and three Cold Packs. The unclean ones will be disposed of rapidly so that they will never be a part of the holy congregation. As the chaff is separated from the precious ore, so will the judgment effect a thorough separation in our midst. Afterwards, it will be the Great Consumption that will celebrate the triumphant church. And so in symbolic fashion I made a purchase of Bareskin Magnum at Panola Pharmacy for the church coming of age in the age of the Pisces!

The Trump Family and the Vanguard of Iniquity.

This family in all their darling dealings take refuge in lies and darkness until the soul bears the impression of evil continually. Trump's 80-foot flagpole at Mar-a lago is a symbol of Babylon and its decadent pleasures. "Therefore the showers have been withholden, and there hath been no latter rain: and thou hadst a whore's forehead, thou refusedst to be ashamed." Jeremiah 3:3

The "van" in the names of the female family members stands for vanguard, the servants of sin in the devil's army. While at the Whitehouse the members chose code-names starting with the 13th letter "M". Mogul for the money representing the god of this world; Mountaineer for the Flintstone Mountain and Marksman for the Gunman. The Muse? Minnie Mouse in heels! No wonder there is a "fanny" in the genealogical line to symbolize the pit!

Thank God that the oppressor hath ceased because his time is up. The vision of the mogul in chains was given to me at Grady in the first volume of Manna. He is chained and we rejoice with rejoicing. "That thou shalt take up this proverb against the king of Babylon, and say, How hath the oppressor ceased! the golden city ceased! Jeremiah.

AMBASSADOR AUDREY MARKS HITS THE "MARK" AND THE WHOLE NINE YARDS.

Ambassador Marks, reigning under the number 13 as Jamaica's 13th ambassador to the United States, is an anointed vessel of God to usher in the year of recompense with her Paymaster, online bill payment enterprise. We are at the billows foam where the unbelieving ones will be destroyed by the slaughter weapons of angels in Ezekiel 9, while the faithful go on to enjoy eternal bliss in Psalm 150. She hails from St. Mary in Jamaica and is the one chosen to be the "womb of the morning" having completed her education at Immaculate Conception High School. We need a change for real and Audrey's moment has come to lead the nations over the great divide into the Promised

Land. We are the forerunners of this kingdom church according to the apostle Paul. "Now then we are ambassadors for Christ, as though God were pleading through us: we implore you on Christ's behalf, be reconciled to God."

Such a reconciliation will be made manifest at the 60th Independence Celebration of Jamaica at the Grand Gala at the National Stadium. We will represent the Christ as the Bridegroom and the church triumphant will be the victorious laity. Jamaica 60 is therefore the Year of Jubilee when the dominion of darkness is overthrown and we take possession of our possessions! We therefore ask for ambassadorial visas to fulfill our roles at the festivities at this most auspicious occasion of Matthew 25. (The Ten Virgins).

And that's the whole 9-yards of the redemption story. We are royalty indeed of the seed and heritage of Abraham our father.

Hallelujah.

Revelation 13:3 "And I saw one of his heads as it had been mortally wounded, and his deadly wound was healed. And all the world wondered after the beast."

But the beast will eventually come to its end as represented in the giant code-blue glove filled to the brim with charcoal grout. A small charcoal ball on top of the glove indicated that the last hand had been played and the "GAME IS OVER!" God is keeping it real. He is not a fictitious God who pulls things out of thin air and asks you to believe Him. He is on the ground and in the trenches to make possible our all powerful deliverance from a powerful enemy. He alone is responsible for our redemption and our transport to the land of promise.

Dominion and power and glory and majesty to the KING of KINGS and LORD of LORDS.

AMEN.

CHAPTER TWO

BAKSHEESH VERSUS BILIOUS

———◦◦◦———

Sabbath May 14, 2022   Time: 3:23 PM

This morning the crows came and assembled on the housetop and on the trees creating the last rite for the SDA church. Sin and the Laodicean church have been put on ice!

There are two rewards to be meted out on the final day, and these rewards are categorized in the Great (baksheesh) and Dreadful (bilious) Day.

Baksheesh means a tip, present or gratuity that originated from *bakhshidam to give; and related to sanskrit bhaksati* **he enjoys. God's great gift to us is encapsulated in the text in John 3:16, "For God so loved the world that he gave his only begotten Son; that whosoever believeth in him should not perish but have everlasting life."**

The righteous will inherit a life of everlasting peace and happiness unlike the unjust who reap the reward of grace in biliousness.

Biliousness: A term used in the 18th and 19th centuries pertaining to **bad digestion, stomach pains, constipation, and excessive flatulence (passing gas).** The quantity or quality of the bile was thought to be at fault for the condition.

Something extremely unpleasant or distasteful is coming on the doorstep of the SDA church like "a long scarf of bilious green."

BELVEDERE SDA CHURCH AND THE FLOATING BED OF ROSES.

Belvedere SDA or the Kirkwood church was the first Seventh-day Adventist church established in Atlanta, during the pioneer years. This is a church that is dedicated to its mission and is intolerant of dissenters. In late 2001, some members objected to my husband's teachings in the Sabbath School class and referred him to the top brass at the Georgia Cumberland Conference who came and dismissed him from the fellowship one Sabbath day. Three years later in 2004, all five leaders of the conference died when the plane they were traveling on, crashed into some trees in the Calhoun hillside near Tennessee. Only a lone survivor lived to tell the tale. I knew this was a retributive judgment because it happened on December 2, which happens to be my first son's birthday. This same date claimed the life of Lowell Hawthorne after he visited Georgia for an Inspirational Luncheon as *The Undercover Boss. (2015).*

The location and address of Belvedere places it at the conjunction of time and destiny because here is where the parting of the ways will begin. The recent spate of deaths at the church was a sounding forth of the death knell for the wider congregation telling them that probation has closed and the sealing was over. The end has come upon the church and there is no escape for her any longer. Ezekiel 7.

3567 Covington Highway,
Decatur, Ga. 30032

The head number **35** references the 35th President JFK, who is a symbol of the first thief on the cross who did not receive the Savior in his heart when he had the chance to do so. He died in his" imminent estate". He lost his soul that day and had nothing to gain thereby. The number **67** is the dividing of **670** by the universal number **10.** The whole number **670** is a combination of the numbers of destruction on the broad road to hell-i-75[D. T] and i-595 [D. H] [75+595= 670]

The zip code that ends in **32** references the 32nd President of the USA, FDR who was a "lukewarm" president even as Belvedere is classified as the Lukewarm church. The enemy of souls wanted us to leave the people alone in their darkness but we prevailed and the Conference can do nothing to silence us now. These dumbdogs that will not bark will be the first to feel the stroke of wrath of an offended God. Even the Georgia Bulldogs have a sharper bark than they do. God left nothing unturned to warn them of danger of keeping quiet in the face of a dangerous predator. Because of the Laodiceans warring against God's truth, this church will eventually become a dunghill once the righteous escape her ranks. You see, the title of the church's Bible Study Guide should be the Shepherd's Rod Series according to Micah 6:9 instead of" Quarterly "which connotes money, moth and rust! They have been feeding on empty stuff all these years that have made them mal-nourished and unfit for the kingdom.

BRIGHTHOUSE AND TAGS.

Yesterday at Aldi I took a box marked Brighthouse to stack my groceries in. The light has come to us in a dazzling array because in the parking lot I found a key tag with the number **054.** This is none other than Abaddon, the Alpha and Omega!

I record many tags as I travel along the highways and byways in Georgia. Some give off positive vibes while others are toxic vibes. Nonetheless I know that it is God active in the masses preparing them for relocation to the land of promise if they are faithful and obedient. He longs to take us out of this sinful, death weary place and establish us on our own hill in Zion. Someone once asked why is there a need for a front and back tag in Jamaica?

On our upward, narrow journey home, the front tag represents the male of the species who is the leader and ruler in the household-the King. The back tag represents the female of the species who follows gently behind-the Queen of the household. She takes that which her husband reflects from the Savior and imparts it to the world. That is why you" read" the woman and not the man." The hand that rocks the cradle rules the world." In this regard she is a priceless commodity!

In America, there is only one tag at the back, indicating that the men are **MIA** [Missing in Action]. Most are quite content in Sodom and Gomorrah with their dicks in chains at the South Bend waiting for sweet release in the bottomless pit. The women wear the pants in the home while the men are queens and queers and dysfunctional homes multiply and you wonder why?

THE FLOATING BED AND ENTERING INTO REST.

The sermon today was centered on Matthew 13:44-46 and dealt with the treasure in the field and the pearl of great price. Pastor made a list of pricey things in the world and mentioned a floating bed. The righteous will rejoice when the get to lie down in their "bed of roses" while the wicked gather about their "bed of thorns".

Lief. (archaic) As happily; as gladly
From Old English *leof* meaning "dear, pleasant; related to the words "leave and love."
Leif. means "heir".
Philippians 4:5 "Let your moderation be known unto all men. The Lord is at hand."

Leif Garrett. Garrett name means strong spear, but here we see a man searching for happiness in all the wrong places! Satan enters our being through the portals of our senses, appealing to our weaknesses and perverted appetites to work the ruin of the human body. One day God is going to take us to the fountain in the land of our forefathers and sprinkle clean water on us so that we will be clean…. He also promised to take away our stony hearts and give us a heart of flesh.

JOHN 17.

THE WORD OF GOD SHALL ENDURE FOREVER. I AM HAPPY BEYOND WORD AS I SEE THE UNFOLDING OF THE TRUTH. THE CHURCH TRIUMPHANT IS LIKE THE FLYING ROLL IN ZECHARIAH'S VISION. [ZECH. 5:1-2]

N. A. P. S
NATIONAL ASSOCIATION FOR PREVENTION OF STARVATION. (sda)

Abundant truth is here for all to partake of in the unfolding of truth. We have the present truth which is meat in due season. "But while men slept, his enemy came and sowed tares among the wheat and went his way." Matthew 13:25-30. The church has turned back from following Christ her Lord and is steadily retreating towards Egypt, yet few are alarmed at their condition. The Belvedere church has been greatly infiltrated by Jesuits. The griseled leadership in the church bears the impress of former president John Donald Trump, the antichrist in Revelation 13. The 3567 address at Belvedere has the configuration of the beast number in 67 where 6+7=13. [9+4=13]. The phone number for Belvedere also bears the Trump numbers of the angel of Laodicea in Revelation 3.

PHONE NUMBER: 404-299-1359

These numbers are primarily odd numbers of imbalance on the matrix. The number **29** in reverse is **92**, the color of darkness. **92-42=50** the Sabbatical Pentecost. **91** represents the combination of Trump's year of birth-'**46** and the number of his presidency-**45**. [**46+45=91**].

The phone number also includes the 35th presidency of JFK in the number 35. The Bay of Pigs represent those who feed at the swine's trough.

The number **13** is a paradoxical number that reveals duplicity in the management of affairs. (Revelation 13 and the Mark of the Beast).

59 is the equivalent to darkness. [5+9=14]God's kingdom sign is expressed in terms of **8+6 or 6+8=14. The kingdom is restored to the saints during the 6th seal, while the 8th division of the church is the purified kingdom.**

There has been great effort at Belvedere to hide the truth from the people and to hide the people from the truth. So, the Belvedere token pen bears the inscription of Trump in the phone number of the church. He is the angel of Laodicea afterall and I don't know whether I should laugh or cry! tRUMP

IS UNMASKED AND THE DEVIL IS EXPOSED FOR WHO HE REALLY IS. WE ARE DELIVERED AT LAST!

The Calrod stove created the 3rd seething pot tonight by burning the soy milk in it to cinders after it boiled over. It was sealed shut and was unable to be unlocked.

Lucky Seven.

God is good and God is great. A seven year old sprinter lost her shoe at the start of the race and ran back for it. She ended up winning the 200 meter dash. God knows no haste and no delay and this chapter is the "Other shoe to drop."

THE ROLLS.

1. Manna: A Consecrated GPS Guide into the Promised Land.
190 pages. Published on February 14, 2020. Price. $13.99
This Book represents the love of God manifested in His word. On the back cover is the barn-the kingdom church into which the righteous are gathered for safety.

The pen name PINNS was used to represent pinnipeds (seals) fin-footed creatures who are messengers of the covenant. PINNS was also used to denote the hairpin that I found in the pew at church today. Hairpin is a U-shaped pin for fastening the hair. Some will have a glorious end while others will meet an inglorious end in the rapture of the wicked. (Ichabod). The sealed ones will make hairpin turns with the gospel to turn the world upside down and rescue souls in Babylon.

2. Manna: Hallelujah to the Lamb of God!
60 pages. Part 8. Price: $10.99
Published on August 4, 2021 to symbolize the Four Winds of Revelation 7,

This Book represents the parting of the waters for the righteous to go through after the judgment hour of Ezekiel 9. The blue color represents the sea of eternity where the redeemed shout hallelujahs of victory.

3. Manna: Aha, Aha. The Narwhals Have Arrived: The Story of the 144,000 Living Saints on the Move!
Pages. 266. Volumes-14, 19&20 Price $20.99
Published on May 10, 2022. The May month represents the Mayflower and starts the countdown of seven literal months to the Great disclosure in the Great and Dreadful Day. The 10-symbolizes universality as in i-Universe Publishing.

This is the Second Exodus Movement. The Lighthouse has come to lead ahead against the enemy. Amen.

4. Manuscript. Unleash the Ride, Motorcycle Show. [2013-2014]

AMEN AND HALLELUJAH, AMEN.

SUNDAY MAY 15, 2022.   **TIME: 5:45 AM**
THE MYSTERY OF GODLINESS REVEALED. THE MYSTERY OF INIQUITY REVEALED.

I received a dream a long time ago where I stood behind former President Barack Obama as he looked intently in the distance. He was watching my husband as the visible king in action at the synagogue of Satan. Through the spoken and written Word my husband got control of the chariot from the mountain and began speeding down i-285 in the brown Camry. (PYB6646). He was going after Trump, the angel of Laodicea to apprehend him. He finally caught him at Grady Hospital and chained him as a prisoner. During the 2020 election debates he was taken to Walter Reed Hospital where he spent 4-days to identify him as the antichrist. Afterwards he was taken to the Whitehouse where he was told to take off his mask and he did so on January 6, 2021 in full display of the Universe. After leaving the capital that day, he was again summoned to the White house where he was beheaded by the White house **NOOSE** and his head given to Kathy Griffin on a platter. The whole hosts of heaven rejoiced at the restoration of all things and King Richard was given a standing ovation as the people hailed David their visible king. When the Philistines saw that their leader Goliath was dead they fled Afghanistan, making a sudden withdrawal after 20-years. Hurrah!

The SDA leadership is very much like the Republicans in Congress in their hostile treatment of those who embrace the Present Truth. Now in the end time they are about to be unmasked and beheaded. God's word cannot lie. After Barack walked away in the dream I went on to behold the Savior skydive to earth and then stood up to deliver us. We are free indeed! Then Isaiah says that the earth shall be full of the knowledge of God as the waters cover the sea. Hence the exalted church has risen up in glory that is why my name Judith Williams is on top of the 3rd Book above the lighthouse whereas on the previous Books the name was at the bottom. Arise and shine for thy light has come and the glory of the Lord is risen upon thee, continues the Gospel prophet.

Over the weekend I placed the **LIFE IS BEAUTIFUL** plaque above the black banded globe in our bedroom to signify the restoration of our Eden home. Eden lost and Eden regained, today.

FROM MOREHOUSE TO THE BRIGHT HOUSE. AT THE END WITH THE MCKENDS. [NEPTUNE]

When I joined the Children's Sabbath School program as the kindergarten teacher, Sister McKend wanted to redecorate the room so she asked her husband to paint it in the colors of his liking. When he was finished we got a clear definition of the separation at Belvedere because the yellow color depicting the wise virgins with the extra oil was at the top while the green color depicting the foolish virgins was beneath. There was a trimmed section with black paint depicting Black gold. In these simple matters those who grow in grace are at last separated from the dwarfs. Those who manifest growth in the christian pathway will be adorned with peacock feathers while the complacent ones will get raven wings. The green on the Jamaican flag run north to south like Esau the Edomite, that was why D. T was killed heading north in the southbound lane. My son moved in the opposite direction on the black line by moving from the east in Kingston to the west in Negril for his bride. The sign for the foolish virgins is the runaway bride from Duluth, Ga. Her truth got dull and she ended up in bankruptcy.

The judgment for the dead message has a seal that carries 59 points, while the judgment of the living has 27 more points reflecting the new birth. The Belvedere phone number ends in 59. (404-299-1359). They have not embraced the additional light.

HERALDS OF THE MORNING.
SAVIORS OF THE WORLD.

Jamaica's 60th Independence celebrations under the theme *Reigniting a Nation For Greatness* is a call for return to the Promised Land. We lost our Eden home and now it is to be restored to us. Marcus Garvey wanted to repatriate the africans back to Africa and that was a noble undertaking. However God is ready to repatriate, not only Africans but the entire globe who are of the seed of Abraham. To this end the only people on the planet who are conversant with Bible history and prophecies regarding this second exodus are the 144,000 living saints who are sealed with the seal of God. They alone have the answers to all the world's crisis and problems because they have the keys to the kingdom eternal. So, we would like the opportunity to make the call at the Grand Gala and offer up the Master's invitation to the Royal Supper or Banquet under the auspices of the Holy Ghost. It will be a call for all nations of earth to gather together in one love in the promised land. Those dictators or better yet "chuptators" had better release God's people that they have been keeping in bondage for centuries or else pay the penalty. China, Russia and Cuba had better know that the sovereign God has come back to set the captives free. God might just manifest His great power and might in this the 5th parabolic year for the tares, so that the world may understand how solemn and important the times we are living in. Get ready. We are here to help you before it is to late! The Neptune army is here and this army is master of the invisible so get ready for show time. We are ready to take charge and we mean it!

PRAISE, HONOR AND GLORY TO THE MOST HIGH. AMEN.

MONDAY MAY 16, 2022.
Fantastik News.

The present truth is here. It is God's gift of salvation to the world. "Thy kingdom come; thy will be done on earth as it is in heaven."
The eye opening truth is here.
The eye popping truth has come.
The kingdom of heaven is at hand.

We need to reignite the Israelite nation and make Jerusalem a holy city once again. Andrew Holness and Sir Patrick Allen are Seventh-day Adventists who stand at the head of the nation to declare that the hour of judgment is come and it starts in the Laodicean church-the very last. A sealed remnant from that church will go on to give the gospel worldwide, calling the people out of false worship to the true God. It's Judgment Morning in America. The leading men in the SDA conferences will be suffering from ED in that day when they see a sword instead of the clouds opening up to receive them into glory! Jeremiah 30:6 "Ask ye now, and see whether a man doth travail with child? Wherefore do I see every man with his hands on his loins, as a woman in travail, and all faces are turned into paleness?"

God has taken the reins in His hands and He will take charge and take care of the flock Himself. He will dismiss the unfaithful shepherds and appoint leaders of His own choosing. My husband's California license reveals he is chosen to lead at long last out of the shadows into the glorious day!

Y-25 penultimate letter
27-Christ's 27 steps to freedom.
77-Perfection. Toots and Maytals age at death on 9-11
74-The 46th president representing the second temple won the elections by 74 electoral votes.
41-This is the color of darkness. Satan is a vanquished foe. He has been canceled in the church.
133- Zaila's Spelling Bee number at the contest in 2021.
13-3 was the 2019 Super Bowl score between the Pats and the Rams.
Revelation 13:3 talks about the whole world who wonders after the beast.
33-Christ's total years of ministry on earth from birth to ascension. He won!

Bundles of joy
The fardel of sin.

God helped me produce two bundles of joy that have brought me immense joy after watching them grow from infancy to manhood. My life was never always an easy journey and they have suffered many things by way of struggles and privations. But they kept their heads high and their focus on God. I pray for them twice every day as I know they are up again a formidable enemy who is seeking their life. But they are anointed and covered from the womb days. Amen

The bundle of iniquity was cleared during 8-turns on the matrix promising to wipe out the wicked root and branch. Craig represents the precious stone in Zion with its swiftness and speed to smite the unjust ones and to smite the nations. He loves to run marathons for charity. Handel represents the return of the tribes and he reflects the reversal of the curse.

We are the great army of reformatory workers who stand at the head of the kingdom church as saviors of the world. We have been anointed and consecrated to our task. We have had our lips touched with live coals from the altar like Isaiah and we come in the spirit of Elijah the Tishbite of old. A fire follows us ahead and behind!

Today I printed a receipt with the exact scores I predicted on the Buccaneers and Chiefs in 2021. Total bill was 31.31 and my score had double 13's in it. [1313 has 31score in it].

So you see, folks, no one has the present truth to dispense to the flock as we do. We know how it is going to end because we have been shown many thing in the revealings of prophecy-the eyes of the church. So let us share the good news of salvation today. We do not want to hear any more sad songs. Enough is enough.

CHAPTER THREE

DREAMS REALLY DO COME TRUE!

Nahum 1:13 "For now will I break his yoke from off thee, and will burst thy bonds ("dons") in sunder.

Isaiah 10:27 "And it shall come to pass in that day, that his burden shall be taken away from off thy shoulder, and his yoke from off thy neck, and the yoke shall be destroyed because of the anointing."

Nahum and Isaiah are saying the same thing that the pressures of living for God's people will soon be alleviated and the world will be level once again. The crooked paths will be straightened and the way cleared for us to go back to the Motherland.

On Sabbath the crows from the landfill came on the roof of the house and in the treetops in the yard as a sure sign of destruction and loss. On Sunday I saw a crushed turtle by the mailbox at the front gate. A sure sign that we have secured our pearl of great price! Sweet Release!

"The flowers appear on the earth; the time of the singing of the birds is come, and the voice of the turtle is heard in the land." Song of Solomon 2:12

It's time for us to get out of the backseat and take charge and mean it.!

THE SHEKINAH GLORY.

It has been an incredible journey from start to finish. Hallelujah and Amen. Thanks be to God our Savior and Deliverer.

"By day the Lord went ahead of them in a pillar of cloud to guide them on their way and by night in a pillar of fire to give them light, so that they could travel by day or night. Neither the pillar of cloud by day nor the pillar of fire by night left its place in front of the people." (Exodus 13:20-22).

"Declare his glory among the nations, his marvelous deeds among all peoples." (1 Chronicles 16:24)

"For God who said," Let the light shine out of darkness. "made his light shine in our hearts to give us the light of the knowledge of God's glory displayed in the face of Christ." (2 Corinthians 4:6)

THE DIVINE PRESENCE OF GOD.

"And I heard a loud voice from the throne saying, "Look! God's dwelling place is now among the people, and he will dwell with them. They will be his people, and God himself will be with them and be their God." Revelation 21:3

REPACK. Definition.

verb. pack (a suitcase or bag again)
b. pack (objects) differently in a container.
In Isaiah 66, we are given the chance to be global missionaries, spreading the gospel of peace through earth's remotest bounds. Hallelujah!

"ONE DAY IT MUS GET BETTA!"

AMEN.

"GIVE ME THIS MOUNTAIN." -Caleb
"GIVE ME THIS HUT." -Leaders at Cohutta Springs.

My little Caleb wanted a Jack-in-the-box for his birthday so we promised him one. Caleb reminded me of faithful Caleb who asked for Hebron mounts as his inheritance. At age 40 he was sent as a spy by Moses to scout out the land of Israel and bring back a report. His Fellow spies brought back a bad report of their inability to retake the land as giant's dwelled there. Forty-five years later at age 85 years Caleb possessed his possessions. Caleb's forty five years are symbolic of forty five U. S Presidents.

Tuesday May 17, 2022.   Time: 6:00 AM

ICHABOD.
GREAT FOR YOU.

The Great and Dreadful Day is upon us. God can no longer tolerate the iniquity workers in the church. He must smite the class of people who are indifferent to His demands for righteousness and clean living. Caleb of old arrived in the Promised Land at age 80 but waited five more years before making his request to take Hebron. The last five years represents the last 5-kings in "the days of these kings." Daniel 2:44 Hence our 40th president Ronald Reagan is a Starting point of the journey from the wilderness to the vineyard. Had he been assassinated in the eighties and another president taken his place, Trump would have been the 46th president instead of the 45th. In like manner had Harriet Tubman replaced president Andrew "Jack and the Beanstalk" Jackson on the $20.00 bill, she would have become the mystery of iniquity number one instead of the rascal. Anyway, once Little Caleb's wish for a Jack-in-the box comes true, Andrew 'Jack and the Beanstalk" Jackson will be put in a box and dashed into a dumpster. Talking about dumpsters, the spiritual dumpster for the Laodiceans is here on the premises with the old Frugals sign my husband made beside it. The inscription of the dumpster has the markings of 9-11. What is actually happening at this stage of the game is the "VIEWING" OF THE SEVENTH-DAY ADVENTIST CHURCH IN THE AGE OF LAODICEA. Read about the "Wake" in Dr. Alonzo Smith's book <u>Abandoned in Brandon.</u> Pgs. 22 and 78. He writes; "The mood of the evening was similar to that of a *"Wake"* as if people had come to pay respects

36

to the dead." There are 56 days between pages 22 and 78 denoting the days the earth takes to cool down after the wicked are burned to ashes. (SR)

DEKALB COUNTY SANITATION.
3SL 19033
404-294-2900

The sinners are on i-294 while the righteous are on i-285 which is the highway to Zion. The repeat of **29** represents destruction as in 9-11. 900 divided by 100=Ezekiel 9 and Apollyon. (Revelation 9) My home address ends in **29 also, making it the 3ʳᵈ such coincidence!** Recently I found my **"NO BUTTON"** <u>**that you press to get a No response to. It signals the day of judgment where the unbelieving ones are given vinegar to drink instead of water to quench their thirst. It will be a time of real anguish and bitterness of spirits.**</u> The number 33 symbolizes Christ's earthly ministry completed and the cross raised up to save mankind from the devil's deathtrap! Those who made the spiritual 10-degree turn on i-75 in Georgia will land on i-85 which in turn becomes i-285 reflecting the second birth. When Caleb of old asked with boldness for the mountain at Hebron, he wanted the kingdom of Israel. Since we are on i-285 it means we must now declare possession of the mountain because the fire passed through on Spaghetti Junction bridge in 2017. The church is victorious and triumphant in its march. It will be joy unspeakable and full of glory; the half has never yet been told.

Those leaders at Ga. Cumberland Conference in Cohutta Springs who insist that there is no kingdom on this earth must realize by now that there is one made up of all nations and tribes of earth. All they will get for their unbelief is an underground "hut" and God's dismissal letter saying "Ta". Utah is the perfect place for those who turn to salt with an "uh-Uh" on their lips. Senator Mitt Romney has measured the time at hand already using Senator Bernie's Mitts and declared that time is up. I never knew that Caleb's age had any connection with i-285, but apparently it does. The 10-unfaithful spies never entered into rest and are symbolized by the awful cry of desperation made by the 5-foolish virgins who came back to the banquet hall when the door was shut. The day is also described by Samuel's daughter-in -law as **ichabod; the glory of the Lord is departed.**

NELSON ROLIHLAHLA MANDELA AND JOSEPH ROBINETE BIDEN.
[LONG WALK TO FREEDOM].

Mandela spent **27 years** in prison, split between Robben Island, Pollsmoor prison and Victor Verster prison. Caleb's wanderings in the wilderness for **40**-years mirrors the captivity of Mandela in the prison for **27** years. [**40+27=67**]. After their wanderings both found freedom-Caleb defeated the giants and gained Hebron, where King David ruled for seven years. Mandela was released from the prison to the palace like Joseph of old. Since, President Joe Biden's middle name closely resembles the prison "Robben" Island it means our status has been upgraded from prison folk to royalty. This is Amazing Grace. Our chains are broken off and we are free! **THE PRISON HOUSE IS EMPTY!**

Another Joe, Joe Scarborough, heralds a new day for us too as he hosts a morning program **MORNING JOE** on MSNBC. Our grievous wound has been healed or Scarborough would not be living in New Canaan with wife Mika. We can now give each other *high-fives* in Connecticut because we are connected to heaven at last and the wicked have been **cut off. The configuration of 67 [6+7=13] means that perfection has come and the end is here. 86 [8+6=14] means that the kingdom has come! Celebrate it!** Jamaica at 60-years marks the year of release where we gather to sing the songs of deliverance and triumph on Mt. Zion. Meanwhile Trump and his allies will head to Sing-Sing and that's not a good thing in the age of Trumpism. But all good things must come to an end, as Sinatra sang at his presidential Inaugural dance; so he has had his full run, and now it's time for him to have the "runs." Hallelujah to the Lamb of God!

When I got home later in the evening, I took up the turtle at the front gate and placed it in the garden. This November my husband and I will be celebrating 37 years of marriage. We got married on a Sunday, November 10, 1985, by Pastor Lewis Blackwell. And Joseph Robinette Biden will be celebrating his second year in office as President of the United States of America. Brighter days are ahead and the best is yet to come! Adios.

Today, Wednesday May 18, 2022
BREAK THROUGH LIGHT. HEAVEN'S LOVE MACHINE. LOVEJOY RECREATION CENTER. COGYRN YOUTH GROUP. WE WILL NEVER PART AGAIN!

Psalm 103:2-5
Bless the Lord, O my soul, and forget not all his benefits: who for giveth all thine iniquities; and health all thy diseases.

Who redeemers thy life from destruction; who crowneth thee with loving kindness and tender mercies; who satisfied thy mouth with good things; so that thy youth is renewed like the eagle's.

Sin's burdensome loan was discharged today.
Satan's envy against God's people has been neutralized by God's forgiveness of all our sins. We are free, after 80 years-the lifespan of a man and the Rod. [1942-2022]. God now sees us as the apple of His eye.

"GOOD FOR NOTHING."

A lesson from the prophet Jeremiah.

When Pris replied to the Master's request "wilt thou be made whole?", with an attitude of self-righteousness, she was used by God to reflect the common disposition of the Laodiceans who say: "I am rich and increased with goods and have need of nothing." Not knowing that they are wretched, miserable, and poor and blind and naked.

Jeremiah was given a lesson from the marred girdle to illustrate the evils of Israel. Israel earned these remarks: "This evil people, which refuse to hear my words, which walk in the imagination of their heart, and walk after other gods, to serve them and to worship them, shall even be as this girdle, which is **good for nothing.** Jeremiah was previously instructed to hide a girdle in a hole of the rock in Euphrates. After many days he went to take the girdle out and it was marred, and profitable for nothing. God intended that the whole house of Israel and the whole house of Judah should cling to Him as a girdle cleaveth to the loins of a man," "that they might be unto me for a people, and for a name, and for a praise, and for a glory: but they would not hear."

Many are deceived into disbelieving the very messages that should save them from disaster until it is too late.

The lesson from the filled bottles.
Jeremiah 13:12, 13. "Therefore thou shalt speak unto them this word; thus saith the Lord God of Israel, Every bottle shall be filled with wine: and they shall say unto thee; Do we not certainly know that every bottle shall be filled with wine? Then shalt thou say unto them; Thus saith the Lord, Behold, I will fill all the inhabitants of the land, even the kings that sit upon David's throne, and the priests, and the prophets, and all the inhabitants of Jerusalem, with drunkenness.

14. And I will dash them one against another, even the fathers and the sons together, saith the Lord: I will not pity, nor spare, nor have mercy, but destroy them."

DOOR DASH.

<u>JustDashit.</u>

The destruction **to come** upon Modern Israel takes place at the Hard Labor Park in Georgia in type. This park was the first one we chose to conduct our **COGYRN YOUTH CAMP. COGYRN** means Camp of God Youth Restoring Network. It was a very fun camp. Here I now see that the unsealed ones in the church-those who when the sealing message came to the church rejected it and refused to sigh and cry for all the abomination done in the midst of the congregation, will be cut down by the angels in hard labor terms.

TOTAL MEMBER INVOLVEMENT. (TMI)

The destruction will involve all SDA church members without the seal of God on a universal scale. (67x10=670)[i-75 and i-595 combined].

"Slay utterly old and young, both maids and little children, and women." Ezekiel 9.

Meanwhile those who escape are transported to Lovejoy ♡ Recreation Center in Atlanta where the heart is renewed and purified and they become priests and kings unto God.

Tags.

TAE. 2387.	Yours for the taking.
CEE 6446.	Behold your King
HA 77 PB.	HAPPY

God cannot bear the separation any longer so He has sent His Son to come and get us. "Son, go get my children from the four winds, from every corner of the globe."

We will never part again. No, never part again. [46. 99].

Bernice's Uncle Andy, The Antitypical Caleb in the Old Testament.

SELMA, ALABAMA.
Job 23: 10 "But he knows the path I take, when he has tried me, I shall come forth as **gold**."

When Ambassador Andrew Young marched in Selma back in the day, his spirit cried out for the mountain of God as Caleb of old did. Like Caleb, he wanted to vindicate God's name and glorify the God of heaven and earth, stamp out the wicked and tread down the oppressors of God's people by the Spirit's sword. He wanted to lift up the downtrodden kingdom in the new world. But back then the mountain he could only view from afar as when Moses stood on Mt. Nebo's heights and viewed the landscape o'er.

However, "Uncle Andy" received his request at age 85 just as Caleb did at 85 years old when he said "Give me this mountain." In 2017, a mountain of fire appeared on I-85, God's purified, spirit filled army and broke the bridge down and engulfed it in fire. The long bondage of sin and darkness has been broken at last. Hebrews 12:29 "For our God is a consuming fire." From the collapse a new bridge emerged in 6- weeks symbolizing a new and living way opened up for mankind. Eighty-five years it took for the mountain of God to be restored. What could this miracle on I-85 at Spaghetti Junction mean other than the kingdom of glory is here and now, i9 and God's presence is residing with us in living form as the **LIVING SPIRIT OF PROPHECY?**

The fire represents the restoration of all things for the faithful. The Tom Moreland Exchange where this occurred was the sign of the fulfillment of the saints having on the exchange garment of Christ's character and His righteousness.

But, Young would wait another 5-years for the mystery of iniquity to be revealed fully in the double impeachment of Trump and the vile insurrection at the Capitol on January 6, so that it would be demonstrated that the mighty God of heaven did cast out the prince of darkness of this world and got rid of the critter so that the oppressed could go free.

BUFFALO
OX-PLOW

Satanic forces are at work to bring misery and woe to mankind as we saw in Buffalo, New York. The sins of the world lie at the door of the church and at 2500 Mt. Carmel Drive, Waco Texas.

God's Heaven's Appeal program is a Loud Cry tool to rescue souls out of Babylon. It deals with fishing and hunting candidates for the heavenly kingdom church and teaching them the oracles found in God's holy words. Heaven's Appeal sends out missionaries two by two as the apostles did in their journeys. No minister should fly solo on these expeditions if it can be avoided. The streamlined approach of Heaven's Appeal will cause the work to explode and belt the earth with the glorious light of the gospel. This is the ox-plow phase of the work we are entering. Only with a purified church, a church freed of sin and sinners can God be able to finish the work and cut it short in righteousness. This formidable kingdom church is able to take on the powers that be and annihilate them. This evening I found an orange tag at Home Depot labeled "Shaded Eye." We have made it safely to the "Bright House." Thanks be to God for Just blessings.

AMEN.

The. End.

Thursday May 18, 2022.   Time: 11:30

RUMOR HAS IT. HE'S BACK! HE HAS COME BACK TO SET THE CAPTIVES FREE.

SAVE THE DATE AND DON'T BE LATE.

IS NOT THE HARVEST THE END OF THE WORLD?
"**The** tares and the wheat are to grow together until the harvest; and the harvest is the end of probationary time…When the work of the gospel is completed, there immediately follows the separation between the good and the evil, and the destiny of each class is forever fixed." Christ Object Lesson pp. 72, 123

"Early Writings, p. 118, reveals that the Third Angel is the one who does the harvesting, while Matthew 13:30 shows also that the angels separate the tares from the wheat "in the time of harvest." Hence Christ's command, "Let both grow together until the harvest," points down to our day, "the time of the end," the period in which the harvest is to be consummated and the "tares" separated from the "wheat."

Thus to all practical purposes "the harvest" is indeed "the end of the world-the end of the wicked."

God is about to punish the men who are settled on their lees: that say in their heart, the Lord will not do good, neither evil. (Zeph. 1: 12).

"I will sift the house of Israel among all nations, like as corn is sifted in a sieve, yet shall not the least grain fall upon the earth. All sinners of My people shall die by the sword, which say, The evil shall not overtake or prevent us." Amos 9: 9

10. "There shall be as the shaking of an olive tree, and as the gleaning grapes when the **vintage** is done. They shall lift up their voice, they shall sing for the majesty of the Lord." Isa. 24:13, 14.

These scriptures show that after the church has been shaken by the Lord's visitation, then her faithful members who are left will "sing for the majesty of the Lord. "The shaking will have made the church what she ought to be." Answerer Book 2 p. 38

On this 19th day of May, 2022 the church's probation is closed and the "tares" bound. This event coincides with the moon turning to blood on May 19, 1830.

On this day on May 19, 2018, Meghan and Prince Harry were married in England representing the second temple restored.

HOT WINGS-WINGLANTA.
REPAIRERS OF THE BREACH. ISAIAH 61.

We have been given the commission to roll back the tide of evil that is threatening to overspread the world at this time. No matter who is placed in the White House, the problems cannot be fixed because God is left out of the plans. The problem of sin cannot be solved by politicians who many times glorify sin rather than rebuke it.

As repairers of the breach in Capitol Hill, we will conduct an anointing service for the desecrated space on Monday July 4, 2022 at 11: 00am. We will pray prayers of consecration and praise in this year of jubilee. As Biden signed Juneteenth into law last year signifying our year of release, so in the second year of his presidency he shall open up the banquet hall for Suppertime for the Bridegroom fulfilling Matthew 25-The marriage supper of the Lamb. In 2017 the Atlanta Falcons scored only 28 points in the Super Bowl against the PATS (34) this after leading with a 25 -point lead and heading into overtime. The "loss" took us to Hallelujah Square at the Banquet Hall in Matthew 25. Amen.

On Sabbath August 6, 2022 at 11:00 AM we will have an anointing service representing the Marriage Supper at Andrews Memorial Church in Hope Road. The old devil is vanquished. The forces of darkness have been beaten back. Let us rejoice and sing. God's quickening power is in the land. We rise up on this day in victory. I signed a copy of Manna: Hallelujah to the Lamb of God. Part 8 for Renee at the store. We have the sacred mission to supply the nations of earth with the living waters of salvation and the living bread of life! The invitation is extended to all. Whosoever Will May come. We are the servants of the Most High hence I wore nursing scrubs to work today!

Measuring with Dr. Palmer, John the Revelator and the Prophet Ezekiel. How do you measure up?

Yesterday we had a discussion about measuring the fruits and vegetables for juicing and the good Doc. said he would come and measure them today! "In the mighty sifting soon to take place, we shall be better able to **measure** the strength [number] of Israel. The signs reveal that the time is near when the Lord will manifest that his fan is in his hand, and he will thoroughly purge his floor." -Testimonies Vol. 5, p. 80

Thus, both the Scriptures and the Spirit of Prophecy proclaim that He Himself will purify the church, and that when she is thus purified, "the Gentiles shall see her righteousness, and all kings her glory." Isa. 62: 2

John the Revelator was given a reed as a Rod to measure. "And there was given me a reed like unto a Rod: and the angel stood, saying, Rise, and measure the temple of God, and the altar and them that worship therein."

This relates to the numbering of the 144,000 living saints.

Mayor Kasim Reed, the 59th mayor of Atlanta was used as a symbol for the numbering of the people. He served two terms from 2010-2018. Thus God measured the temple during his tenure. As the 59th mayor he takes us to the end of the Judgement of the Dead message and the beginning of the Judgement for the Living. [59+27=86]. (Revelation 11.)

Reed was succeeded by Mayor Keisha Lance Bottoms. During this time, those who were measured [numbered] but did not measure up were cut off by the sword. [Lance]. Keisha's name means "Great joy" and depicts the great joy the saints will feel when they escape the great and dreadful day. (2018-2022)

Lance Bottoms was succeeded by Andre Dickens who exemplifies our great expectations met. The ones cast out and trodden underfoot are told "ta-ta" by Felicia Moore the Atlanta council member opponent whom Dickens defeated. It's over and done!

The prophet Ezekiel was shown the Mighty River of Ezekiel 47 to show the progression of the work from a tiny rivulet to a wide body of water that could not be crossed except to swim across. "And when the man that had the line in his hand went forth eastward, he measured a thousand cubits, he brought me through the waters; the waters were to the ankles."

The gospel flowing like a mighty River will bring healing to our world. On the bank of the River were trees for meat and the leaves for medicine.

Today the electronic sign for the Ornaldo Swift Health and Wellness Clinic and the Frugals Health Food store was installed at the entrance on Snapfinger woods Drive. We hail it as the cross being lifted up to save to the uttermost parts of the earth. "One day, a worker from Courts Cabinetry came over and asked us if we had seen the green panels for making shelves anywhere. We told him "no" although he really came to tell us that we have the green light now to enter His courts this Thanksgiving. Indeed, The mighty River of Ezekiel 47 could well be named Kissimmee because righteousness and peace hath kissed each other today." Psalm 85.

We exalt the great name of our Lord and King.

ZOOM............. ZOOM............... ZOOM!
MATLOCK STANDS FOR: THE WELCOME *MAT* AND THE DOOR IS *LOCK(ED)*.

The Investigative judgment acts upon one's case after his life's career in relation to salvation has ended. The SDA's life's career has ended. Jennifer Wilbanks, the Runaway Bride, represents the Laodicean church at harvest time who came back too late to the door of hope. She cried out, "The harvest is past, the summer is ended and (we) are not saved." Jeremiah 8: 20. Her alter ego Halyna Hutchins had to pay the penalty by friendly fire on the set of Rust in Albuquerque. Pat Tillman was killed by that same friendly fire while on duty in Afghanistan. The wages of sin is death and the kiss of death looks just like when Rush Limbaugh of Fox fame gave "24" actor Mary Lynn Rajsskub a kiss on the lips before he died. Rush died at age 70 years in 2021 and the winds are about to be let loose. [70+"24"=94] [9+4=13].

While the 5-foolish virgins let out cries of anguish in Bonanza, the 5-wise virgins shout "bonanza" in Bonanza.

Of course Matlock saw them soaring up like birds to Peachtree in Atlanta and rejoiced that they got their $38.00 tickets for JAYWALKING by a policeman on duty. Therefore Atlanta is where the shouts of victory are to be heard first and foremost.

"Thou art worthy, O Lord, to receive glory and honor and power: for thou hast created all things, and for thy pleasure they are and were created." Revelation 4:11

Christ came and fought for our estate and won. The old trickster has run out of chances and must now pay with his very life. This too will be his waterloo.

Blessed be the throne of God forever.

Amen.

Friday May 20, 2022.   Time: 5:34

WHATEVER IS NOT OF FAITH IS SIN. THOSE WITH THE GREATEST FAITH WILL FEAR THE LEAST.

Esau Found No Place For Repentance.

"And the songs in the temple will be howling on that day." Amos.

Those without the seal are kept in place at Sing Sing Correctional Facility in New York, where they will be singing "the blues."

Jesus is our Best Friend on Best Friend Rd. in Georgia. The shooting at a Tops Friendly Market store, in Buffalo, New York was a confrontation with darkness.

The Spirit of Truth has left Minnesota and George Floyd's demise to establish Himself in the Kingsley neighborhood in the city. While in Minneapolis, at the Cups Food grocery store, God handed Jeremiah a cup. "For thus saith the Lord God of Israel unto me; Take the wine cup of this fury at my hand, and cause all the nations, to whom I send thee to drink it. So I took the cup at the Lord's hand and made all the nations drink, to whom the Lord had sent me." Jeremiah 25:15-16

God has unleashed His fury on the wicked inhabitants of earth to destroy them.

Report: On May 14, 2022, a mass shooting occurred in Buffalo, New York at a Tops Friendly Market store, a supermarket in the Kingsley neighborhood on the eastern side of the city.

18-year old Payton S. Gendron carried out the dastardly deed while livestreaming on Twitch.

Our estate has been restored to us by the great sacrifice of Christ on Mt. Calvary. The name Gendron means "son-in-law and that means that God is here to restore the family relations. Do not fear those who kill the body and when they are done have nothing more to kill: but rather fear Him who can cast both body and soul into hell. We will not fear in a world that has already been conquered! It's the top of the hour. Can you see your Bestie now?

T. G. I. F (THANK GOD IT'S FRIDAY.)

The ignominy of Christ's suffering on the cross elevated us to the throne of heaven. We die daily to self and crucify the natural man so the image of God can shine through.

Licking the Globe.
Slang.
    a.   to beat or thrash
    b.   to defeat soundly: licked their rivals at Lacrosse.
We have been "licked into shape" by many stripes, struggles and suffering. We are better for having endured the chastening of God.

EAT CROW.
Phrase of crow.
Informal. North American be humiliated by having to admit one's defeats or mistakes.

Eating crow is a colloquial idiom, used in some English speaking countries, that means humiliation by admitting having been wrong after taking a strong position. The crow is a carrion-eater that is presumably repulsive to eat in the same way that being proven wrong might be emotionally hard to swallow.

The 5-foolish virgins "eat crow" in the end.

-Wikipedia.

Buffalo soldiers and Buff Bay Portland in Buffalo New York.

Our pilgrimage in a strange land is about to end as our Heavenly Father comes to gather us home to the Motherland where we were stolen from. The

Buffalo is a wild ox or bison of the bovine family that epitomizes strength, the ability to overcome adversity and the will to survive!

Through God's amazing grace we have overcome the Enemy. [Hoover-Comey]. We have made it to port in BuffBay Portland where the naked truth shines forth in splendor. We are prophecy "buffs" and are able to guide you safely to the shore. Behold the sun is shining through so do not be disbelieving.

Philippians 2:10 "That at the name of Jesus every knee should bow, if things in heaven, and things in earth, and things under the earth."

The Buffalo also describes something mystical and powerful. It also means to overawe or intimidate someone. I guess the naked truth is now ready to take on the gospel work in this ox-plow stage of the game and finish the work of the gospel in all the earth. This May well be the year for the real thing!

TAGS.

1. **F-150 TDX. 0054. Cut off point.**
2. **EVH 126 FL. Eve's House restoration completed.**
3. **EQJ 180. The great equalizer 180 degrees.**

And so, the house of Hagar-a house of bondage, represented by "427" has been dissolved today while the spiritual house of Sarah was restored in the birth of L. P on 10-27. Flesh and blood cannot inherit the kingdom of God so only the converted will be allowed admission. The kingdom door is open, come inside my friends. You are My friends and I love you! Of course the Baksheesh tip jar is what holds the tip of eternal life and our pearl of great price. It is the Food Depot of Joseph's day. Frugals Health Food Store and Deli. (2022). Hallelujah.

When I got home in the evening, I found an **Omni spark ignition wire set** box that my hubby discarded so I took it up. This poor old world has been groaning for a change long enough and now is time for action!

HERE COMES LIGHT THROUGH DARKNESS. The Great Controversy, Chapter 19.

My Baksheesh Tip Jar.

Revelation 22:12 "And, behold I come quickly; and my reward is with me to give every man according as his work shall be."

God did give me a generous tip today of a penny reward symbolizing eternal life. The 144,000 first fruits are sealed and saved. Matthew 20. The first shall be the last and the last shall be first.

We give thanks forever more.

Praise be to the Most High. Amen.
Sabbath May 22, 2022
Ez.

A DAY TO CELEBRATE TEA.

Tea.

1. a hot drink made by infusing the dried crushed leaves of the tea plant in boiling water.
4. Informal. US
Secret information or rumors of a scandalous nature; gossip
Origin. Chinese *te* related to Mandarin *char*.
Char.
Partially burn (an object) so as to blacken its surface. [charcoal].
Ecclesiastes 12:14 "For God shall bring every work into judgment, with every secret thing, whether it be good, or whether it be evil."

The light will exclude the evil workers of darkness.

Portions of the Tribes and of the Sanctuary. Ezekiel 48.
Ezekiel 48:1 &2 "Now these are the names of the tribes. From the north end to the coast of the way of Hethlon, as one goeth to Hamath, Hazarenan,

the border of Damascus northward, to the coast of Hamath; for these are his sides east and west; a portion for Dan."

"And by the border of Dan, from the east side unto the west; a portion for Dan."

Living in exile in the 6ᵗʰ century BCE, the prophet has a vision for the restoration of Israel.

Siege of Jericho. The Walls Fall.

This morning at Sabbath school, after studying Matthew 25, the parable of the 10-virgins we saw the Bridegroom appear on screen. "And at midnight there was a cry made, Behold, the bridegroom cometh; go ye out to meet him." Matthew 25:6 He was dressed in a blue shirt. So, we circled Jericho's wall 13 times and at the last shout the walls of partition fell down flat.

"So the people shouted when the priest's blew with the trumpets: and it came to pass, when the people heard the sound of the trumpet, and the people shouted with a great shout, and the wall fell down flat, so that the people went up into the city, every man straight before him, and they took the city."

PROMISES TO THE PENITENT ONES.

Isaiah 57:13-21. "When thou criest, let thy companies deliver thee; but the wind shall carry them all away: vanity shall take them: but he that putteth his trust in me shall possess the land, and shall inherit my holy mountain; And shall say, Cast ye up, cast ye up, prepare the way, take the stumbling block out of the way of my people. For thus saith the high and lofty One that inhabiteth eternity, whose name is holy; I dwell in the high and holy place, with him also that is of a contrite and humble spirit, to revive the spirit of the humble, and to revive the heart of the contrite ones. For I will not contend forever, neither will I be always wroth: for the spirit should fail before me, and the souls which I have made. For the iniquity of his covetousness was I wroth, and smote him: I hid me, and was wroth, and he went on forwardly in the way of his heart. I have seen his ways, and will heal him: I will lead him also, and restore comforts unto him and to his mourners. I create the fruit of the lips; Peace, peace to him that is far off, and to him that is near, saith the lord; and I will heal him. But the wicked are like the troubled sea, when it cannot rest, whose waters cast up mire and dirt. There is no peace, saith my God, to the wicked."

This reversal of fortunes reminds me of the Prince and the Pauper story, that is akin to the story of Esau and Jacob; that is akin to the story of Norbert and his friend. His friend lived large while Norbert suffered many privations because of theft.

As life turned out, the friend has no peace in his life now because of certain choices. Norbert as crowned king can have the peace of God now having seen the light at the end of the tunnel. I present to you all, David, the visible King.

Zophar shows the state and portion of the wicked.

Job 20.

"Though his excellency mount up to the heavens, and his head reach unto the clouds; Yet he shall perish forever like his own dung: they which have seen him shall say, "Where is he?"

He shall fly away as a dream, and shall not be found: yea, he shall be chased away as a vision of the night. The eye which saw him shall see him no more; neither shall his place anymore behold him. He hath swallowed down riches, and he shall vomit them up again: God shall cast them out of his belly. He shall suck the poison of Amos: the viper's tongue shall slay him. He shall not see the rivers, the floods, the brooks of honey and butter. That which he labored for shall he restore, and shall not swallowed it down: according to his substance shall the **restitution** be, and he shall not rejoice therein. Because he hath oppressed and hath forsaken the poor; because he hath violently taken away an house which he builder not; Surely he shall not feel quietness in his belly, he shall not save of that which he desired. He shall flee from the iron weapon, and the bow of **steel** shall strike him through. It is drawn, and cometh out of the body; yea, the **glittering sword** cometh out of his gall: terrors are upon him. All darkness shall be hid in his secret places: a fire not blown shall consume him; it shall go ill with him that is left in the tabernacle. The increase of his house shall depart, and his goods shall flow away in the day of his wrath. This is the portion of a wicked man from God, [Bro. L] and the heritage appointed unto him by God."

Only with our eyes shall we behold and see the reward of the wicked!

WE HAVE ARRIVED. WELCOME HOME.

REVELATION 21:12-14

"And had a wall great and high, and had twelve gates, and at the gates twelve angels, and names written thereon, which are the names of the twelve tribes of the children of Israel; On the east three gates; on the north three gates; on the south three gates; and on the west three gates. And all the wall of the city had twelve foundations, and in them the names of the twelve apostles of the Lamb."

TOP to BOTTOM with KEISHA LANCE_BOTTOMS.

Ezekiel 31:3 "Behold, the Assyrian was a cedar in Lebanon with fair branches, and with a **shadowing shroud**, and of an high stature; and his **top** was among the thick boughs."

In verse **13** we see the demise of this lofty nation as predicted by Ezekiel. "Upon his ruins shall all the fowls of heaven remain, and all the beasts of the field shall be upon his branches."

War News forecast is what the world should be getting to help save antitypical Nineveh from ruin in the modern era. Everything is now in position for the last deep strife. The veil in the temple has been rented in twain from top to bottom in the following events. Our Father is about to conduct a D-day assault against Mother and those without the seal are about to perish like "rats in a sewer."

"And, Behold, the veil of the temple was rent in twain from the top to the bottom; and the earth did quake, and the rocks rent; Matthew 27:51

Christ turned up at the bottom of the hour in Minneapolis with the killing of George Floyd at 8:46 am at CUp Foods. Then He turned up at Tops Friendly Market at 2:30 central time at the top of the hour. Fourteen people in all were killed in both incidents. (1+13=14). 8:46 am means quarter to nine. Keisha's name meaning "Her life, and "Great Joy", as the 60th mayor of Atlanta brings an end to all things in the 60 minutes of the judgment hour. "Weeping may endure for a night, but joy comes in the morning." (Psalm 30:5)

Here Christ has come back with His reward in giving His saints a **crown** and to the wicked He gives a **frown**!

We Love You Lord. Amen.

CHAPTER FOUR

MR SKETCH SCENTED
(A sweet perfume is upon the breeze)

―――――●○○○●―――――

At the Tops Friendly Market in Buffalo, an employee phoned 9-11 when the shooting started, calling for help. The 9-11 operator asked her why she was whispering? She did not want to give away her location. But that whisper was the whispering of the angels bringing tidings of good news that the purification of the church is not far hence. No more will the unclean ones pass through us. Let the glory of the Lord rise among us; Let the praises of our King rise among us; Let the songs of the Lord rise among us: Let the joy of our King rise among us!

DANCE
Until the stars
Come down
From the sky

Canaan's land is just in sight against the backdrop of these tumultuous times.

TROUBLE.

The day of doom is shortening its shadows, and we are face to face to face with the most momentous issues to face a generation of men. We hear the footsteps of an approaching God.

Our Captain is here and we are [prepared]for battle, to this end. "Truly the light is sweet, and a pleasant thing it is for the eyes to behold the sun:" Ecclesiastes 11:7

Amen.

BRUCK OUT! BRUCK OUT!

Sunday, May 21, 2022." Time: 5:20 AM

A ROYAL HOUSE ESTABLISHED. —

We conducted the prayer service this morning using Job 19. "And though after worms destroy this body, yet in my flesh shall I see God. Whom I shall see for myself, and not another, though my reins be consumed within me."

Our darkness will turn to everlasting day as we cash in on our inheritance made available at the cross. [EBT-Electronic Benefit Transfer].

THE FALSE SHEPHERDS REMOVED.

Jeremiah 23:1 "Woe to the pastors that destroy and scatter my sheep of My pasture! saith the Lord."

Ezekiel 34:2 "Son of man, prophesy against the shepherds of Israel; prophesy and say unto them, woe be to the shepherds of Israel that do feed themselves! Should not the shepherd feed the flock."

Jeremiah 50:6 "My people hath been lost sheep: their shepherds have caused them to go astray, they have turned them away in the mountains: they have gone from mountain to hill, they have forgotten their resting place."

God will discharge these unfaithful shepherds from service and install His servant David instead. This one shepherd will accomplish what a multitude failed to do.

Ezekiel 37:24, 25 "And David my servant shall be king over them; and they all shall have one shepherd: They shall also walk in my judgements, and observe my statues, and do them. And they shall dwell in the land that I have given unto Jacob my servant, wherein your fathers have dwelt; and they shall dwell therein even they, and their children, and their children's children for ever; and my servant David shall be their prince forever."

This David brings SMART HELP to the picture so we can outsmart the Devil. "And shall make him of quick understanding in the fear of the Lord: and he shall not judge after the sight of his eyes, neither reprove after the hearing of his ears. But with righteousness shall he judge the poor, and reprove with equity for the meek of the earth: and he shall smite the earth with the Rod of his mouth, and with the breath of his lips shall he slay the wicked." Isaiah 11:3&4

ROUGHNECKS. OIL DRILLING INDUSTRY.

(virtually unbeatable).

We sink the shaft deep into the mine of truth so that we may walk safely in this vile and crooked world.

Prayer for succor.

Psalm 44:23 Awake, why sleepest thou, O Lord? arise, cast us not off forever. Wherefore hidest thou thy face, and forgettest our affliction and our oppression? For our soul is bowed down to the dust: our belly cleaveth unto the earth. Arise for our help, and redeem us for thy mercies' sake."

BEHOLD YOUR KING!

Grand Slam in Paris. The Parting of the Ways.

A great reformatory army of workers is about to burst on the scene of action. It was the French general Berthier who took the Pope prisoner that brought an end to the Dark Ages. The church must be cleansed before it can undertake the divine task.

In 2002-2003 I was in the Bahamas on a teaching expedition. When I came back to the U. S the Old Man on the mountain in New Hampshire fell. Within 5-years in 2008, the first Black President was elected in an historic election. In 2019 an epic hurricane devastated the Abaco islands in the Bahamas. 2003-2019. In 3-short years after on my 58th birthday and the Grand Superbowl in Sofi stadium between the Rams and the Cincinnati Bengals, the temple was cleansed. (19 years total rotations) 2003-2022.

Those Seventh day Adventists who disbelieve the Testimonies and refuse to sigh and cry will perish in the general destruction at the hands of the angels when they come to slay. Only thus can the work be cut short in righteousness and the people delivered from bondage!

The End.

Monday Morning May 23, 2022.

My mother's birthday is today, May 23. She would have been 88. My husband and I planted flowers and amaryllis at the store in her honor. Thanks be to God who has gently led us to Green Pastures. 🌸🌷🌺🏵️🌼🌻🍀▢ Amen and Amen.

Empresses came for relief from a chest cold and hubby made a liver flush juice for her which she liked. Mingled with prayers and praise it worked wonders. We live in a broken world and we all need healing in the restoration of the kingdom church. We made the cut today!

Christ's remedy is the efficacious blood that cleanses from all sin and the manna that nourishes the soul and keeps away diseases. To this end a kingdom has been prepared for the faithful to seek redemption.

The System.

I was invited to a Black writers group on zoom yesterday and "Zion" was so happy I went to hear stories written by my peers. Lady R reflected on how she was dismissed from her hospital job because of downsizing. It was the manner in which it was done that worked the most harm to a diligent worker. She went to work as usual and was then called into the office and told to pack her things. Her friend knew about the firing, but she was told to keep quiet or she would be fired also! This vile type of dismissal happened to me in the Bahamas as a way for the Assyrians to take vengeance on God's people. The Assyrians have a yoke around the neck of God's people but by the grace of God, it is broken today! Blood! Fire, Brimstone! for all the oppressors in Babylon.

Oracabessa and the head of gold. [cabeza].

Since Ambassador Audrey Marks is from St. Mary, her name "Marks", corresponds to the image beast of Revelation 13, in Oracabessa. This head of gold system will demand worship of all nations to a false god and those who defy the requirements will be marked for death. Thanks be to God that great multitudes will come out and be saved.

Shortwood College in Cherry Gardens.

When we got flooded out of our apartment in Wolverton in 2011, we stayed at Comfort Inn Suites for a few days. That Sabbath while we were heading up the elevators after church service, a man took off his Rasta cap and gave it to Norbert saying he liked how he talked in a deep and strong voice as he was greeted. We were very impressed. That weekend was the same weekend that Kate and William got married and we watched with delight as they walked down the aisle. That was eleven years ago and God wants us to rejoice because Kate symbolizes the First Solomon temple now "back in the middle!" Her son George represents Adam, the farmer in his garden while Prince Loui represents the 5th FBI director Loui. Freeh. Cry For Freedom. Princess Charlotte is the feminine version of Charles, a "free man."

And so, on their 11ᵗʰ wedding anniversary, they visited Jamaica and Shortwood Teachers' College, my alma mater as a witness that the darkness of earth is over and mankind is free. You see Shortwood is located in the Cherry Gardens area of Norbrook where the Great Consummation takes place. (11+11=22) Revelation 22.

The last time we saw the light it gave us courage. I purchased two barrels today from the shipping company where Steve works who was a coworker of mine. We have enough barrels of truth to fill Lucas Oil stadium 10-times over!

The Bermuda Triangle [Devil's Triangle].

- o **Florida** (Tampa Bay Buccaneers)
- o NFL
  - **Puerto Rico**
  - Paper towel throw a party.
  The valley of **Achor For** a **Door** of hope.
  - **Bermuda**
  - Joined together as one
  - Clear Day
  - Sin cut short in righteousness [Bermuda shorts]
  - The dumb shout hosanna and the deaf hear His name.
  - Bermuda grass and the green, green grass of home.

Labor Day in Jamaica JM.

The labor of love Christ undertook to redeem us has paid rich dividends. I placed a 1964 penny in my tip jar representing eternal life, the reward of the saints. I am filled with joy unspeakable and full of glory.

Now the earth is quiet and at rest and at the 23ʳᵈ Session of our Movement in Waco, Texas I will testify and sing "God is truly amazing."

Thanks be to our Father eternal. Amen.

The "Bee's Knees"

My hubby's knees.

Potato 🥚 Head is the set locked outside the door. God has the seal locking instructions under His belt. This truth is to belt the world with righteousness much like Atlanta's beltline in north -west.

Present truth is what the flock needs.

When Shadrach, Meshac and Abendigo were put in a burning fiery furnace like the modern Kilauea volcano in Babylon, they survived because they had extra oil that extended their lives. You can come under that same divine protection by adhering to the truth. The truth will set you free.

Amen.

Tuesday, May 24, 2022. Time: 9:26 AM

Amos eight and the basket of summer fruits.
Senator Hillary Clinton and the "basket of deplorables".
Ambassador Audrey Marks "weighs in" on the three decrees.

Yesterday, I received an email from the Ambassador Audrey Marks thanking me for the soft copy of my last Book: Manna: Aha, Aha! The Narwhals have arrived. (The story of the 144,000 living saints on the move!)

What a movie in store for all! She agreed with the comment made that without vision the people perish.

But later on two emails were sent saying a recall was made on the previous email and it left me saddened and disappointed. Only thing it was a mistake!

Yet in that mistake the Ambassador became the voice of God, issuing commendations to the first fruits of Harvest-the 144,000 living saints with a large vision and issuing a stark condemnation for the baskets of deplorables that Senator Hillary named on her campaign. The recall notice could well be a quote from Amos: "Thus hath the Lord shewed unto me; and behold a basket of summer fruit. And he said, Amos, what sweat thou? And I said, A basket of summer fruit. Then said the Lord unto me, The end is come upon my people of Israel; I will not again pass by them anymore." Amos 8:1&2T. The recall notification was equivalent to the 3 decrees of Ezra when a death decree was issued to anyone hindering the building of the temple. In our time the death takes out the offending ones who tarnish the beauty of the purified church.

RECALL.

1. bring (a fact, event, or situation) back to one's mind; remember.
2. officially order (someone) to return to a place.

"The Panamanian ambassador was recalled from Peru."

- (of a manufacturer) requests all purchasers of a certain product to return it, as the result of the discovery of a fault.
- the removal of an elected government official from office by a petition followed by voting.
- bring (someone) out of a state of inattention or reverie.

God is calling us back to our home in the Middle East and when that happens it will be like we are in a dream. "When the Lord turned again the captivity of Zion, we were like men that dream."

Idiom. **beyond recall**

In such a way that restoration is impossible.

The Laodiceans who rejected the Present Truth message are *beyond recall* today.

Ambassador Marks then brings closure to our situation and Dr. G. Marks from Trinidad and Tobago handed us our gladiator sword and our marching orders. We have cut ourselves from the father of lies (trinity of deceit) and have taken the chariot into all the world. **Tobago-*In*[TO]all the world the [Bay] horses [Go]! Zechariah 6.** I have written 6-volumes representative of the 6th seal in which the kingdom is restored. All in all there are 4-Books of varying degrees of intensity.

Such is our great deliverance that calls for rejoicing today. We are at peace and are complete in Him. John 15:13 "Greater love hath no man than this, that a man lay down his life for his friends."

Indeed we are His friends.

So those who play the fool and lose their souls are like a "Jack-in-the Box figure.

Then here is the label for the ones recalled in the church.

They are bound and out in a Haplag container for Dallas, Tx. where they exclaim "alas, alas, the harvest is past, the summer is ended and we are not saved. Jer. 8:20. Notice that there are 24 containers, the amount of hours in a day and 10-Po# denoting a universal number.

So, we give thanks for the accuracy and simplicity of the word. What a hullabaloo!

Amen & Amen.

"Horse Gone Through the Gate".

High Five!

Zechariah 14:20 "In that day shall there be upon the bells of the horses, **Holiness Unto the Lord;** and the pots in the Lord's house shall be like the bowls before the altar."

A holy and great people is described here. Prime Minister Andrew Holness from the tribe of Gad represents the unfolding of the truth that espouses holiness. He has carried the torch high, providing housing in every area for the "homeless" and needy.

These receipts forecast the riches and eternal wealth of the kingdom church.

Frugals

- $38.88(Renee)
- $17.27 (Miss T&T)
- $4.64. (Me)

It is time to celebrate our victory with a High-Five!

Hallelujah, Amen. Thanks be to God.

Wednesday, May 25, 2022. Time: 11:46 A. M

Timely Greetings and Christ's Greetings.

Yesterday, I made a haystack grout stone in a salad container with a snow-white cross in the middle with a gold head-band at the side. This represents the final triumph of the cross which has led us from the lowly stable in Bethlehem, to the palace at the White-House.

I wore a www. greekflix. com T-shirt to work today and stopped by the Milk & Honey restaurant to take a few pictures before I headed to Home-Depot to make some light-bulb purchases. When I got back to the store it was a delight to have customers from church as first purchasers for the day. It was a real joy to serve them as they represented a sampling of the first-fruits of harvest-time. This very morning too, I received three copies of my latest book- Manna: Aha, Aha! The Narwhals Have Arrived. (The Story of the 144,000 Living Saints on the Move).

On page 119 of this Book is a record of the "Kool Cat "and the 144,000 living saints escaping destruction of a plane crash in Sweeden. It was quite something to discover how we could have done that!

Texas.

Nineteen children and two adults were killed when a gunman opened fire in a Texas elementary school on Tuesday, according to the Texas Department of Public Safety.

John 10:10 -17. "The thief comes only to steal and kill and destroy. I came that they may have life and have it abundantly. I am the good shepherd. The good shepherd lays down his life for the sheep. He who is a hired hand and not a shepherd, who does not own the sheep, sees the wolf coming and leaves the sheep and flees, and the wolf snatches them and scatters them. He flees because he is a hired hand and cares nothing for the sheep. I am the good shepherd. I know my own and my own know me, just as the Father knows me and I know the Father; and I lay down my life for the sheep. And I have other sheep that are not of this fold. I must bring them also, and they will listen to my voice. So there will be one flock, one shepherd."

Satan is the thief and great usurper who has been consolidating his forces for a long time to destroy mankind. The 18-year old shooter was acting under the directives of this master general at **ROBB** Elementary to show his malice and envy towards those who have unmasked and thwarted his purposes in the earth. Satan is a loser! He has been soundly defeated and brought down low by the Living Word. Nelson R. Mandela left **ROBBEN** Island a free man to take his place at the palace in South Africa. Joe **ROBINETTE** Biden's presidency is one that shines a light in the darkened places as he declared that joy in the morning is here and now, at his inauguration, fulfilling John 2:19-21.

ROBB elementary, therefore is the gushing out of sin in its final course of the display of evil.

Christmas in July 4, 2022 (USA).
Christmas in August 6, 2022 (Jamaica).

Under the directives of the Holy Spirit, we would like to take our high, exalted responsibility to task by organizing an anointing service at the U. S Capitol to heal the breach that was created on January 6, 2021. We will rally the tribes to repair the breach and sound forth the proclamation for a return to the land of our fathers in Mt. Zion. The same anointing service will be done at a national level in Jamaica on August 6. Let us rise up and seize the day and beat back the forces of darkness once and for all! A Great revival and reformation is needed in the land!

We are at the very brink of disaster, and to delay in these matters is inviting more trouble and distress.

The kingdom doors are open and the initiation is extended to one and all. There is a brand new world awaiting the faithful where no heartaches and pain will be experienced at all. We will be happy, contented, and joyful. Indeed our Eden home will be restored to us forever- a kingdom of mortals.

1 Corinthians 2:9 "But as it is written, Eye hath not seen, nor ear heard, neither have entered into the heart of man, the things which God hath prepared for them that love him."

Thanks be to God our King. We are ready to "Fill a Bag" and help feed families with the gospel message that alone can save to the utmost!

Amen.

CONCLUSION

The signs have been speaking to us in clear tones so all we have to do is pay attention and listen carefully. These are solemn times but if we follow on to meet our Savior we will experience real freedom and the birth of a new day.

May God bless and keep everyone. It may be difficult but help is on the way. Everything is gonna be alright.

Thursday, May 26, 2022   Time: 11:05

God on the "Warnock" Path.
Straight into the bosom of Abraham & Ossoff.
"Robber" caught @ last! "Beto" day comes @last!

God works in a mysterious way, His wonders to perform. God has unraveled the darkness by using signs, symbols, numbers and codes so that we can lighten up our world and bring the truth to understanding. We have followed Him through the sanctuary (Thy way O Lord is in the sanctuary. Psalm 77:13) and now at journey's end He wants us to "lighten up."

The Millerite Movement suffered great disappointment when they gave the last warning to the world and waited for their Lord to come: "Come, Lord Jesus, and come quickly." But He had not come. This disappointment however was not so great as that experienced by the disciples at Christ's first advent. They had shouted "Hosanna to the son of David" in joyful anticipation of His ascendancy to the throne, yet in a few days they witnessed His agonizing death and laid Him in the tomb.

When Christ arose from the grave they were able to perceive all that the prophets had foretold and "that Christ must needs have suffered, and risen again from the dead." Acts 17:3

Miller stated later on," Although I have been twice disappointed. my hope in the coming of Christ is as strong as ever." GC.p407

God's 10-degree turn from Sandy Hook (Connecticut) to Robbs Elementary (Texas).

So, in the fullness of time God revealed in His spirits the last 10 years to the Great and Dreadful day of God. (2012-2022)

A shooter, 20-year old Adam Lanza from Adams shot and killed 26 people. This shooting occurred on the birthday of James Comey, 7th FBI Director, on December 14. It signaled that the Savior had come suddenly to His temple since Comey represents the seventh and last of the churches of Asia Minor. This sudden coming was foretold by Malachi when the Lord appears suddenly to purify the sons of Levi and cleanse His temple. The kingdom came with this coming because Comey is the height of this kingdom, measuring 6 ft and 8 inches (6+8=14) and the 5th joining of the state of Connecticut to the Union symbolizes "High-Fives." The righteous were "let off the hook" in that moment and forgiven all their sins. They rejoice and give praises to their Lord and King. In New town, God was doing a new thing in separating the "tares" from the "wheat" and putting the "wheat" in the Barn. We are in the promised land in the bosom of Father Abraham and Ossoff.

God had also determined that *"by hook or by crook"* He was going to let the "Robber" know that was *on the hook* for all the devastation wrought on the earth. This "Robber", *as crooked as a barrel of fish hooks*, must now know that his 15-minutes of fame are up as designated by the Connecticut State route number 15.

The "Robber's" expiration date was given to him at two football games in 2017. In the 2017 game between Ga. Bulldogs and rival Alabama, Alabama won with 26 points and Georgia lost with 23 points. In 2017, at Lucas oil stadium match-up between the San-Francisco 49er's and the Colts, the scores were the same with the 49er's winning with 26 points and the colts with 23. The repetition of "49" score will surely bring about the cleansing of the sanctuary in short order. No wonder V.P Pence "hooked it" when he heard the sirens of heaven blaring at Colt stadium.

Certainly, God has taken the reins in His hands and He is leading although it may not appear so to us. He will *hook up* with the five wise virgins in a cool connection while He cuts off the ungodly and the abominable.

The Climax in Texas.

The state of Texas, known as the Lone Star state is a prominent wing of the Papacy in Rome. You can always substitute the "fallen star" for a "wolf" and you would never know the difference! The Governor Abbott, whose name means "Father" is but an instrument of Rome. Notice how school shootings and gun violence increased during his tenure and this state was the first to enact abortion laws in the country.

However, we can say that a "Beto" day is on the horizon because yesterday at the 23rd Session at 2500 Mt. Carmel Dr. sin finally ran its course when the "Robber" was caught *hook, line and sinker* at Robb Elementary with the publication of Manna: Aha, Aha. The Narwhals Have Arrived. (The Story of the 144,000 Living Saints on the Move!).

The great light shone and extinguished the serpent and his activities. It was on yesterday that I received a call about the best enema solution for a cancer patient. We recommended the coffee high retention enema as that also tells us to wake *up and smell the coffee* in the spiritual realm.

The Waterloo sign for the unbelievers came in floodings by my work station at the shop because of buckets of water overflowing the area.

Yes, our God is not experimenting because at the gas station this morning I found a red knob gadget that symbolizes the capture of sin. (**PXR 090917**) **The number 9 is the number for completeness. The Devil has exhausted his options and he has been out-maneuvered by the Champion Lion of the Tribe of Judah. The supply chain has been cut! Daniel 8:14 "And he** said unto me, unto two thousand and three hundred days; then shall the sanctuary be cleansed."

To illustrate that the light has come at last, I wrapped my hubby's stack of boards at the shop in a yellow plastic wrap since I could not find the clear plastic ones. Then I rolled the yellow wrap into a ball and labeled it with tags[0564]and[10000149368] These are kingdom and earthwide numbers manifesting the purification of the church.

So, there is a Promised Land and this feels like home to me.

The Answer, the Cure and the Anointing.

Someone asked this question: "What are other countries doing differently to prevent mass shooting of their children, other than just having police running to the schools after the crime, calling press conference, and announcing **breaking news? (Same O) (#7)** Blood is on your hands, your heads and your shoulders.

We 144,000 living saints have the answer and the cure to this world's maladies. We would like to perform an anointing service to repair the breach at the U.S capitol and the Jamaica National Arena. This great army of Reformatory workers would like to pray in the spirit and power of Elijah to bring about a restoration of the once downtrodden kingdom. Politicians cannot solve sin problems with mechanical tools as only the sword of the spirit can cut off the head of the Goliath of today and set God's people free. With this anointing, mass school shootings **will be a thing of the past.** Death will be a thing of the past. Crime and violence will be a thing of the past and accidents too. A fountain will be opened to the **House of David** for sin and uncleanness which will make sickness and suffering, a thing of the past. Zechariah 13:1. Officer Sicknick's death was a sign exposing the sickness of those in darkness. This anointing will usher in the pre-millennial kingdom of eternal peace and happiness. Ask Usher whose daughter Sovereign has just announced that the sovereign **God is here. (Isaiah 54).**

AMAZING GRACE HOW SWEET THE SOUND.
HALLELUJAH TO THE LAMB OF GOD.

A PROCLAMATION!

3429 River Road
Decatur, Ga.30034
May 28, 2022.

Her Excellency, Ambassador Audrey Marks:
1520 New Hampshire
Ave. North West,#7
Washington, DC 20036.

Zechariah 4:6 "Then he answered and spake unto me, saying," This is the word of the Lord unto Zerubbabel, saying, Not by might nor by power, but by My Spirit," saith the Lord of hosts.

I do hope that all is well with you and your family. I thank you for your tireless dedication and love in helping humanity.

I have written four books that are books of enlightenment in a world of disarray and would like to share them with you. (1) Manna: A Consecrated GPS Guide into the Promised Land. (2) Manna: Hallelujah to the Lamb of God! (3) Manna: Aha, Aha. The Narwhals Have Arrived! (The story of the 144,000 Living Saints on the Move! And (4) Manna: Unleash The Ride.Motorcycle Shows.com (2013-2014).

They may seem a lot, but I receive these enlightenments in a timely fashion so that I would not be confused on my journey. I realize now that God has indeed anointed you for this post as the 13th Ambassador to date. Your appointment fulfills the Revelation 13, prophecy where a "mark" is given to those who accept the Mark of the Beast, and also fulfills Ezekiel 9, where a "mark" or seal of deliverance is given to the faithful. Yours is no ordinary mission.

Everything in our world today is in a state of agitation and I would like to provide a solution to the problem by using Divine intervention. In analyzing the recent school shooting in Uvalde Elementary School in Texas, Tucker Carlson of Fox News said this: "A person who is intent on committing violence is hard to stop under any circumstances. An act of Congress isn't going to do it. Neither will gun control." [me: **but I know a Man who can!**]

Someone called him out as a liar. But why is it that for years these things do happen and the police run to the schools, call a press conference and announce *Breaking News on all t.v networks?*

We are a great army of reformatory workers who know as well as Tucker Carlson does that there is no power on earth other than the "sword of the Spirit" that can cut off the head of the Goliath of today. We are aroused by these things to" put on the whole armor of God, and to take the "sword of the Spirit.(Ephesians 6:11, 17). This sword is a neutralizing force, as it offers "smart help." Therefore we would love the opportunity to conduct an anointing service featured as "Christmas in July", at the Capitol, on Independence Day, July 4, 2022 to repair the breach and beat back the forces of darkness. **The sins of the world's impenitents lie at the door of the church.** Officer Sicknick, who died in the riots of January 6. was a symbol of the open wound in the nation that needs healing the world over. We have the saving balm that the world so longs to hear-a message that the kingdom of heaven is at hand and the Promised Land is in view. This is the gospel truth and we have the kingdom keys. We will have the little ones pray and lift up their voices too to help our cause. The people need to come out of Babylon and leave off the works of iniquity before God rains down the seven last plagues in her domain. Revelation 13.17. We have a message of good news that will help the people come under divine protection and escape the destruction soon to burst upon the world.

The theme for *JAMAICA 60, REIGNITING A NATION FOR GREATNESS* is a response to God's voice through the prophet Isaiah "to arise and shine." When Jamaica shall have reached 60-years, sin would have run its course in the church hence the Tribe of Judah (for most Jamaicans are from the Tribe of Judah) must mount up with wings as eagles and run with the gospel message of peace that the once down-trodden kingdom is rising to prominence and peace. God is inviting all nations of earth to come to this kingdom church and be free. Prime minister Holness therefore represents Israel as "holiness unto the Lord." He is from the tribe of Gad however, whose name means happiness, fortune and luck because he is an overcomer. You, Her Excellency is from the tribe of Ruben who represents the excellency of dignity and the excellency of power. The Hispanics are primarily from the tribe of Zebulon, while the Asians are from Napthali tribe. No wonder we Jamaicans have as our motto: "Out of Many, We are One" because we embrace the world as one family and it's one love.

And so this kingdom church: <u>The Victory Church @ Mount Zion's Land,</u> would also like to carry out an anointing service dubbed "Christmas in August "at the National Arena on August 6, Independence Day. Under this anointing, we will under the auspices of the Holy Ghost make school mass shootings a thing of the past. Sickness, pain and suffering will also become a thing of the past. Death will be a thing of the past as we are living saints. The craving after sin will be a thing of the past because in this kingdom there will be a fountain opened to the House of David for sin and uncleanness. We will have a craving for righteousness instead. Homelessness will also be a thing of the past as Amanda Gorman stated that every man will be under his own fig tree. Micah 4:4. Ha, and former President Trump and trumpism will be a thing of the past.

Please give us the opportunity to make these changes in our world once and for all. The old Devil knows that this message will chain him for a thousand years and reduce his being to ashes as if he never was, hence he is furious and behaving like a roaring lion seeking whom he may devour.

I must say that these promises may sound incredible and too good to be true but they will come to pass because our mighty God never does what is possible, but the impossible!

May the peace of God abide with you and your family. Amen.

Sincerely Yours,
Judith A. Williams.

God makes a ten-degree turn in Newtown, Connecticut to UValde in Texas and "the other shoe drops."
And the declaration was sent forth throughout the whole realm of Laodicea that "It is Done."

This morning I found a label in my apron pocket that read: *Unwrap Adventure Sweepstakes.ActivateRewards.com. Open Here.*

It made me even happier when I found two **DELTA labels** with instructions for faucet installation, one in yellow and the other in white. Later on I also picked out a **SORRY card from the box with the number one (1) saying Move forward. We are the first fruits.** I couldn't be happier as this card was labeled to spell the separation that is soon to take place in the church. And once we left home and traveled 400 yards we saw a line of vultures on the road feasting on a deer that got killed overnight.

Destruction comes to the wicked suddenly and unexpectedly.

Sandy Hook Elementary-Robb Elementary.

Sandy Hook is associated with the 7th FBI Director James Comey, because the mass shooting took place on his birthday and he represents the last division of the church-Laodicea. Robb Elementary is associated with the fourth FBI Director William Steel Sessions because the judgment is now in session and the mass shooting targeted fourth graders and teachers. The **UV** at the beginning of Uvalde stands for ultra-violet rays and the **U** forms the word *aulde or old*. So Robb Elementary School is really the shortened form of The **OLD ROBBER** Satan who has come to steal, kill and destroy. Satan presents himself as a savior and kind benefactor to mankind but under this concealment he hides a deadly intent. Salvador Ramos was used as his instrument to destroy lifes and create havoc and pain. Who can stop this Goliath? He is but the **anti-christ in this age and Christ will chain him. Yes, Christ has caught the Robber at long last.**

The old Devil hates the light and the truths that will chain him to the bottomless pit because he hates to be unmasked. But the light has come to us and we rejoice in its splendor. Texas is a "Vatican State" where the father of lies resides. Baby Jessica fell into a well in Texas, illustrating our helplessness in the face of evil. We cannot redeem ourselves as only God can. It was in Texas that Juneteenth was established, giving freedom to the slaves who were unaware that they were free! The Jasper Byrd and Botham killings took place in Texas while the Elk fire destroyed over 80-lives in 1993. When the ERCOT snow storm blanketed the state and wiped out electricity for millions of households it was a sign of judgment day. The winter of sin and the end of the harvest were in view.

The people are fast asleep in their errors and sins and they need to be awakened to their danger before it is eternally too late.

The two eighteen year old killers are telling us that we have come full circle (360-degrees) and the end has come upon the church. In the spiritual realm, the Salvador Ramos shooter could represent the angels that have come to slay those who eat their defiled bread in the congregation. The 4th grade represents the Hagar's House of Bondage that got dissolved that day. The Leaders of the SDA conferences had only gotten in their possession the seal for the Judgment for the Dead message which is equivalent to $59.00, so their congregations must pay with their blood the balance of $27.00 to total $86.00 even for the Judgment of the Living.

So, on May 24, 2022 the house of Hagar was separated from the house of Sarah and the branches and palms and rams celebrated the escape from Bozrah. [86-23=63] Isaiah 63.

The numbers of the Robb Elementary shooting fit the timeline of the 1977 Linjeflyg flight 618 crash in Stockholm, Sweden. Nineteen passengers and three crew were killed in the crash numbering 22, while at the school, nineteen children were killed, two teachers and the perpetrator were killed, also numbering 22. [19+22=41]

Nineteen years ago, I left Nassau, Bahamas and that represented nineteen rotations that closed down the gates of hell. [2003-2019-2022]

The Oracles of God.
The Ark of Safety.

My family was chosen and entrusted with the Word of God in earthen vessels. Nonetheless it is the pure unadulterated Word that has been preserved for posterity, and has safeguarded us over dark and dangerous terrain.

The mystery of the vision- "most startling revelations" coincide with our birthdays and the release dates of the books.

1. Shepherd's Rod Volume one
     255-pages
December 1930. (Craig and Pris)

2. Shepherd's Rod Volume two
     304-pages
September 1932.(Norbert)

3. Volume Three. Timely Greetings and Tracts
     898 pages
June 9. (Caleb)

4. Manna: Volume one
     190 pages
February 14, 2022 (Judith)

5. Manna: Part 8
     60 pages
August 4, 2022 (Shiloh)

6. Manna: Volumes 14, 19&20
     266 pages
May 10, 2022 (Ethan)

7. Manna: Manna: Volume 21
July 2022 (Handel)

There were eight people saved in the ark in Noah's day, and today we have eight people as representatives of the First -fruits in our day. Tomorrow is Memorial Day and I give God thanks for His awesome revelations and triumph over wrong! It is time to have a real Holiday! What do you say?

Amen.

MEMORIAL DAY.   **MONDAY MAY 30, 2022**

AT THE TABLE OF BROTHERHOOD IN THE KINGDOM. INFINITE WISDOM HAS LED US THROUGH THE SAVAGE SEA OF SIN INTO THE VINEYARD OF OUR GOD. AMEN. Our Redemption is complete. Grace and peace be unto our Savior.

Psalm 23.

The Lord is my Shepherd, I shall not want. He maketh me to lie down in green pastures: he leadeth me beside the still waters.

He restoreth my soul: he leadeth me in the paths of righteousness for his name's sake.

Yea, though I walk through the valley of the shadow of death, I will fear no evil: for thou art with me; thy Rod and thy staff they comfort me.

Thou preparest a table before me in the presence of mine enemies: thou anointed my head with oil; my cup runneth over.

Surely goodness and mercy shall follow me all the days of my life: and I will dwell in the house of the Lord forever.

THE ROTTEN TIMBERS REMOVED.

My niece S.S was laid to rest in Westmoreland yesterday signaling the removal of the rotten timbers in our midst. She was like the bad fish caught in the net that had to be cast out. As her mother Ms. F. strayed from the true paths of life so this young lady strayed and brought forth the dead fruits of fornication to light in a miscarriage.

And so, as Norbert cut down the Mimosa tree in the front yard after the service, so are the wicked no more to pass through us. Amen.

Those who have not come under the transforming influence of God, those who are clothed in their filthy garments, those who have not been washed in the blood of the Lamb will be shut out of the kingdom. The self righteous ones amongst us will not "make the cut."

Let No Man Take Your Crown 👑.
Show time in Missouri. The Great Disclosure.
Going To the Chapel and We're Gonna Get Married!

Today as we headed out to the Tile shop and Laundromat, I saw a red gas bottle in the road near the cross walk. It reminded me of the 5-foolish virgins who went back to get extra oil but were eventually destroyed. Then as we entered the Chapel Hill community I saw a Gregory & Levett and Son hearse heading in the opposite direction. For those without the seal Christ says: "Let's just kiss and say goodbye!"

At the SDA's 61st General Conference Session the theme is: **JESUS IS COMING. GET INVOLVED.** Since we are in Missouri, the show me state, we will show the Adventists that Jesus has already returned in His invisible form in the person of His saints- the 144,000 servants of the Most High. We are already disclosed to view in a four-fold series of books called Manna. The Laodiceans conflated the signs of the second coming of Christ with the signs of the coming kingdom of mortals. That was why in 2020 they were barred from Lucas Oil Stadium where they hoped to have kept their 60th General Conference Session. So in 2022 they pivoted to Missouri in June where in 2005 they held their Session under the theme: **Transformed in Christ.** The transformation period for the saints is passed and gone in this harvest time.

As my husband and I worked on the green boards a coworker asked us to do, I could not help but think of the green landfill for the lost and the lovely green pastures for the saved of earth. The massive Missouri Arch in St. Louis is a representative of Adams Clan Restored and Healed.

JOHN WESLEY RINGS WEDDING BELLS OF GRACE.

Wesley Chapel in Decatur is a symbol of the **chapel of love**. Here we see that God's grace is sufficient to save us from the demon's power. Today the church and the Bridegroom exchanged "I Do's" with the Shirelles.

"Certificate of Cleanliness."

I went to the Laundromat to pick up the certificate of cleanliness given to the redeemed. In the first round, I used the number 9 washer that had already been paid for. Then I used Dryer number 41 for 30 minutes. Pastor G. paid $30.00 for the Half-an -hour silence on Friday, 27th May.

The next two washers were #16 and #12 and the Dryers used were #40, 39, & 38 loaded in that order.

The number 38 dryer represents the 38th President of the United States Gerald Rudolf Ford formerly Leslie Lynch King. This latter name means that the kingdom of mortals has a king and a sword to execute judgement in the earth. Christ Himself will carry out this dreadful work according to Ezekiel 9. Nebraska where Ford was born teaches us to ask for whatever we need from our Heavenly Father. He granted a *presidential pardon to Richard Nixon* for his role in the Watergate scandal. It was a controversial move but he was satisfied that he did the right thing. During Ford's senior year at University of Michigan a controversy developed when Georgia Tech said that it would not play a scheduled game with Michigan if a black player named Willis Ward took the field. Ford was Ward's best friend on the team. He planned to withdraw but Ward encouraged him to play. This is what a kingdom of mortals will look like in the Promised Land. In his swearing in address as president he said that he had not sought this enormous responsibility, "but I will not shirk it."

He also stated:" My fellow Americans, our long national nightmare is over. Our Constitution works; our great Republic is a government of laws and not of men. Here, the people rule. But there is a higher Power, by whatever name we honor Him, who ordains not only righteousness but love, not only justice but mercy...let us restore the golden rule to our political process, and let brotherly love purge our hearts of suspicion and hate."

As this mighty general spoke down the annals of history to our day May we in glad triumph say today: Our long national nightmare is over. Sin and sinners are no more.[at least in the church.] The 37ᵗʰ President Nixon *[The Crook]* therefore was a type of the Laodicean church (SDA) flooded with "Tares" and the unconverted. The old dragon spewed water out of his big dragon mouth to carry away the church. But we defeated him and are liberated to take the gospel of the kingdom to our fellowmen in bondage. Let us rise up and greet the day of new beginnings as Justice Sandra Day O'connor would have us do. El Paso, where she lived had seen the Word come to pass- it's a new, glorious, bright, happy, triumphant, fair, illustrious, glad, and marvelous day! Who knew the number 38 held such magic!

We are in the pink today. The church is finally reunited with her Lord today. God wants us to awake and be alert to the signs of the times. Freddie Gray's death should stir us to use our gray matter so that the devil won't deceive us. There is ample provision made in the Word of God for our success so do not trifle with your birth right. Know your rights! While I was parked at the Laundromat a Kenan tanker came to refill the Chevron gas station and parked really close to my van. I figured that the source of all goodness and light had come into the house today.

Let us get the love fest going on from now and henceforth. We have cleaned out the darkness and unraveled the forces of iniquity by numbering them to destruction. Let us rejoice. And so, as Renzo Cameron witnessed the rising up of the truth to the skies in the receipt of a manuscript in the first month April, even so in the second month of May, R.T will witness the fall and destruction of the tares in the church on the arrival of another manuscript. You see, once Flores arrived in Pittsburgh and handed Kobe Bryan-the Mamba his number 24, it blew him out of the skies in his helicopter, along with his 13-year old daughter in 2020. The "lake of fire" Revelation 19:20, is as real as real can be even if you attend the Catholic Church every Sunday.

When we got home a fierce wind blew among the trees and the rain fell for a short period of time. These were showers of blessings.

The journey is now complete. Hallelujah, Amen.

Tuesday, May 31st, 2022   The Last Day. The Last Time. 6:46 AM

So, yesterday, we washed all our troubles away at the laundromat and the curtains of the temple were clean and dry. I can hear Queen Bey singing in my dreams, **AT LAST!**

Handel our son **did a business transaction for us on Memorial Day that would help to free us up financially in the long run.**

So the consummation took place last night and I was glad. Amen.

So Send I You. So send I you to bear My cross with patience,

And then one day with joy to lay it down,

To hear My voice, "Well done, My faithful servant-Come, share My throne, My kingdom, and My crown!"

"As the Father hath sent Me, So send I you."

Total Member Involvement (TMI) means that it is the laity not the leadership that God will use to finish the work of the gospel in all the earth. A purified Layman's Movement will close the gospel work and usher in a world of peace and harmony after all.

Now is the time for us to Meet the Press (CBS) and Face the Nation. (NBC).

HALLELUJAH TO THE LAMB OF GOD!

Printed in the United States
by Baker & Taylor Publisher Services

This book highlights current events and interprets them in the light of Inspiration. There is a real war going on between the forces of light and the forces of darkness and these are not mimic battles. They are as real as the armies of earth in combat with the opponent. We are at the parting of the ways in our departure to the Holy Land and the Enemy of souls wants to hinder your progress. We do not know where the serpent has laid his traps except as we follow what Inspiration says in the revealed Word. Hence a deep study of the truth will give you great insight and offer divine protection so that you can save your soul from destruction which is sure to come.

The book manipulates time lines and symbols to show the nearness of time with astounding accuracy. Words and numbers create light because numbers do not lie! So in an age of floating rumors and lies, please rely on this Book to tell you the whole truth because you will know the truth and the truth will set you free. As you walk through these pages you will realize that it's all over for the wicked forces while for the righteous our Jubilee has just started. These promises are real and we will be rewarded double for all our troubles. The end of our long tiring journey is here.!

Judith Williams is the author Manna: A Consecrated GPS Guide into the Promised Land and Manna: Hallelujah to the Lamb of God. She studied at the Shortwood Teachers College where she developed a love for words in Spanish and Linguistic classes. She was raised in the sleepy town of Frankfield, Nestled in the Bill Head mountain range. She never ever imagined herself as a writer, but when she began receiving vivid dreams and visions relating to the end times she knew she had to share the information with the world. Judith lives with her husband Norbert in Georgia and she has two adult sons.

ISBN 978-1-6655-6150-1